Careers in Counseling and Psychology for Masters Level Graduates
A Guide to Choosing the Right Career Path

Edited by Dr. Audrey Lucas
Bowie State University

cognella
San Diego, CA

First published in the United States of America in 2010 by Cognella, a division of University Readers, Inc.

Trademark Notice: Product or corporate names may be trademarks or registered trademarks, and are used only for identification and explanation without intent to infringe.

14 13 12 11 10   1 2 3 4 5

Printed in the United States of America

ISBN: 978-1-935551-04-1

www.cognella.com 800.200.3908

About the Authors

Cubie A. Bragg, Ph.D., DAC, NCC., L. I. C. S.W., LCPC is a licensed counselor and psychotherapist. He holds a Ph. D. in clinical psychology, and he is a full-time faculty member in the Department of Counseling at Bowie State University. He is also Director of the Adler-Dreikurs Institute of Human Services and coordinator of the Adlerian Counseling Psychology Program at Bowie State University. He is an internationally known lecturer, and a national doctoral addiction counselor and therapist. He is certified by the National Board for Certified Counselors, Inc., and is a Licensed Independent Clinical Social Worker in the District of Columbia. Dr. Bragg has completed extensive research in stress management, depression and anxiety disorders. He serves as a reviewer for several national journals and is the recipient of numerous awards for his outstanding work with youth and child care workers. Dr. Bragg is Owner and Chief Executive Officer of Bragg Training Consultants. He has published independently, with peers and graduate students. He has also co-authored conference papers, thesis manuals, developed new courses, and written grants. He currently serves on various boards of directors and committees at Bowie State University and the community at large. He continues to present scholarly papers at several professional conferences and maintains applied skills via consulting in his areas of expertise.

Kimberly M. Daniel, Ph.D. is Assistant Professor and Coordinator of the School Psychology Program at Bowie State University. She obtained her Bachelor of Science Degree from Howard University. She completed her graduate training at The Pennsylvania State University where she obtained her Ph.D. in School Psychology. Dr. Daniel has worked as a School Psychologist in the Pennsylvania and Maryland public school systems for 16 years. Dr. Daniel is a state certified Maryland School Psychologist and a Licensed Psychologist in the District of Columbia. Dr. Daniel holds active memberships in the Maryland School Psychologists' Association, National Association of School Psychologists, American Psychological Association, and Trainers of School Psychologists. Currently she manages the daily activities of the School Psychology program at Bowie State. Dr. Daniel has taught several courses including: School Assessment, School Based Consultation, Psychological and Educational Interventions, Counseling in the Schools, Practicum and Internship. Dr. Daniel's research interests include topics such as school consultation and problem-solving practices in urban settings, the impact of depression on learning, pre-referral intervention practices at the secondary level, parent training, and the impact of ADHD on learning in higher education.

Karina Golden, Ph.D. is an Associate Professor at Bowie State University in the Department of Counseling. She received her doctorate in Counseling and Development from The American University. She has a Masters of Arts in Literature and a Bachelor of Arts in English/ Writing & Philosophy.

Dr. Golden is a poet, psychotherapist and educator who specializes in creative approaches to healing including: Jungian archetypal psychology, poetry therapy, spirituality, mind-body medicine, dreams and fairy tale interpretation. She is a former board member of the Washington Society for Jungian Psychology, The National Association for Poetry Therapy, and the Maryland Association for Counseling and Development. She currently serves with the Baltimore Jung Working Group and is conducting research on creative approaches to counseling. Dr. Golden's interests include poetry and school counseling. She has published many works and is a member of several professional organizations.

Rosalyn V. Green, Ph.D. is an Assistant Professor at Bowie State University in Bowie, Md. with a Ph.D. in Counseling Psychology. Her area of expertise in the Counseling arena is with couples, families, and groups. Dr. Green teaches Family Counseling, Group Counseling, and Marital Therapy. She is also a licensed and ordained Reverend in her church and is thus able to bring the relationship between theology and psychology into the therapeutic setting. Besides teaching and preaching, Dr. Green also has her own private practice and is very active within and outside her community by presenting at workshops, seminars, retreats and other such environments. Her passion is to empower and challenge herself and others to grow, change, and thrive to live life to its fullest potential. Dr. Green has recently published her first book entitled "Our Father: Imprints that shape our lives."

Rhonda Jeter-Twilley, Ph.D. is currently an Associate Professor and Chair of the Department of Counseling at Bowie State University. She earned her Bachelor of Science degree in Communications and Theatre Arts with a minor in English at Taylor University. Dr. Jeter-Twilley taught for three years at the junior high and high school levels in Philadelphia. She earned a Master's degree in Family and Community Development specializing in Family Therapy at the University of Maryland-College Park in 1984. Subsequently she received her Ph.D. in Professional and Scientific Psychology from the University of Pennsylvania in 1995. Dr. Jeter-Twilley taught at the University of Maryland Eastern Shore for ten years in the Master's Program in Guidance and Counseling. Four of those years she served as the Coordinator of that program. During the 1998–1999 academic years, she was a Visiting Assistant Professor at The George Washington University. Dr. Jeter-Twilley does research and has presented nationally, regionally, and locally on current topics in the counseling field. Some of her areas of expertise include: counselor supervision, relationship issues, conflict resolution, mentoring, women's issues, group process, racial socialization, racial identity, and dissertation completion. Dr. Jeter-Twilley is credentialed as a Certified Secondary School Teacher,

National Certified Counselor, National Certified Psychologist, and a Licensed Certified Professional Counselor.

Jake Johnson, Ed.D. is an Associate Professor in and past department chair of the Department of Counseling in the College of Education at Bowie State University. He is a Licensed Professional Counselor, a Licensed Clinical Professional Counselor, a Nationally Certified Counselor, trainer, consultant, educator and author. He teachers graduate courses in school counseling, mental health counseling and counseling psychology and supervises the practicum and internship in school counseling. Professionally, he is an active member of the American Counseling Association (ACA). In ACA, Dr. Johnson has chaired, participated and presented in sessions and workshops on creating a healthy workplace, stress management, rage, diversity, multiculturalism, existentialism, and existential cross-cultural counseling at national and international conferences. He is also an active member of the Association for Multicultural Counseling and Development (AMCD): Past-Chair, Association Development; Co-chair, Twentieth Anniversary Committee; and Past-Chair, Twenty Fifth Anniversary. He is a Past-President of the Maryland Association for Multicultural Counseling and Development (MAMCD), and a Past-President, Maryland Association for Counseling and Development (MACD) and currently serving as a board member. Dr. Johnson is a board member of the International Center for the Study of Psychiatry and Psychology (ICSPP).

Audrey A. Lucas, Ph.D. is an Assistant Professor at Bowie State University and the current editor of this book. She holds a doctoral degree in Educational Psychology and a Master of Arts in Counseling Psychology. She is a licensed School Psychologist in the District of Columbia, a Licensed Clinical Professional Counselor in the State of Maryland and a Certified Family Therapist. Dr. Lucas has extensive experience working with at risk student populations in K-12 and at the University level. She worked as a school psychologist for 8 years providing assessment and counseling services for both Elementary and High School students. Dr. Lucas served as the Acting Associate Dean for Special Student Services at Howard University from 2002–2003. She has six years of experience at the University level working as an academic advisor and psychological counselor at both Bowie State University and Howard University. Dr. Lucas is currently the Coordinator of the Professional School Counseling Program at Bowie State University where she holds a fulltime faculty position. Dr. Lucas has presented both locally and nationally on topics such as student retention, working with urban parents and dropout prevention. She is advisor to Chi Sigma Iota, and a member of the Maryland School Counseling Association, the American School Counseling Association, National Association of School Psychologists and the American Educational Research Association. Her research interests are centered on the cognitive and emotional development and assessment of children and adolescents.

Frank Norton, Ph.D. is an Associate Professor in the Department of Counseling at Bowie State University. obtained his doctor of philosophy. (1976) and M.A. (1972) in clinical psychology from the University of Denver and earned his B.A. in psychology from the University of Massachusetts, Amherst campus. He is past chair of two departments of psychology and past director of an American Psychological Association (APA) approved clinical psychology doctoral internship. Also, he served as clinical director of a hospital inpatient alcohol program and has worked with dual diagnosed patients in private practice. For the past 14 years, he has taught full time in the Department of Counseling at Bowie State University. Currently, he is their coordinator of the Mental Health Counseling Master of Arts program and also has developed a graduate level Certificate in Addictions program.

Henry J. Raymond, Sr. Ph.D. is a Full Professor in the Department of Counseling, College of Education, Bowie State University, Bowie, MD. He received his doctorate in Counselor Education from the George

Washington University, Washington, DC. He is a National Certified Counselor and received post-doctoral training Human Resources Development from University Associates in California. He teaches or has taught most of the graduate courses of counseling in the Counseling Psychology program within the Department of Counseling including group counseling, Adlerian Theory and Practice, Life Style Assessment, Legal and Ethical Issues in Therapy. His is one of the co-founders of the Alfred Adler Institute of Human Relations at Bowie State University.

Jennifer West, Ph.D. is an Assistant Professor in the Department of Counseling at Bowie State University. She earned a Bachelor of Arts degree from Howard University where she graduated Phi Beta Kappa and Magna Cum Laude. She earned a Masters of Science degree in Clinical Psychology from Towson State University, and her Doctorate of Philosophy in Education and Psychology from the University of Michigan with a specialty in School Psychology. Dr. West is a Nationally Certified School Psychologist and Licensed in the state of Maryland. Dr. West is currently an Assistant Professor at Bowie State University and brings 15 years of professional school based experience to the program. She was formerly the Psychologist for Achievement Equity for the Howard County Public School System. In that role, she utilized a Research, Development and Demonstration model to help the school system accelerate the achievement of student populations performing furthest away from local and state achievement standards. Her research interests are focused on the relationship between culture, cognition and achievement, particularly among ethnic minority and economically disadvantaged students. Her primary courses include: Introduction in School Psychology, School Based Consultation, Cultural Proficiency in School Psychology, Child Psychopathology, Seminar in School Psychology; Practicum in School Psychology II.

Otis Williams, III, Ph.D. is an Assistant Professor at Bowie State University in the Department of Counseling. He received a Ph.D. in counseling psychology from Howard University and a M.S. from Johns

Hopkins University. Dr. Williams completed his clinical internship with the Maryland State Department of Public Safety and Correctional Services, where he provided clinical services for both male and female inmates. Later, he worked as a mental health clinician with the Maryland State Department of Juvenile Services. Prior to his academic appointment at Bowie State University, Dr. Williams served as an adjunct professor at Johns Hopkins University. His research interests include substance abuse treatment with African American inmates, social justice issues and counseling, traditional African religion/spirituality, and racism-related stress and coping. He is the co-author of several research articles published in professional journals.

Contents

Preface

This book is intended to assist current graduate students; those interested in a graduate degree in the fields of counseling and psychology and those who have graduated from a graduate program in counseling and psychology gain the information necessary to choose the appropriate career path.

Graduate schools offer academic training in a variety of counseling and psychology disciplines, such as: counseling psychology, school psychology, mental health counseling, school counseling and etc. At the graduate level it is most expedient for students to choose a discipline at the beginning of their program. Delays and changes after the first or second semester can prove to be very costly and time consuming. Most graduate programs offer open houses and information sessions, provide information about their degree offerings through their website and provide faculty advisement to students interested in pursuing careers in counseling and psychology. Unfortunately, these informational opportunities do not prevent students from making changes and preparing for professions that don't really suit their professional goals, personalities or life styles. Most students enter the field of counseling and psychology with great enthusiasm, conviction and direction, some students enter unsure of what opportunities will be available upon graduation. Some students who do choose a career are unaware of the licensure requirements, roles and responsibilities, and specific training needed for that career.

In search for a guide to assist students in gaining the knowledge they need about opportunities after graduation, there were very few resource guides found. Many books discuss best practices in certain fields, professional development in certain areas and licensure and certification requirements in response to current legislation, but few provide enough information on career options after completing graduate studies in counseling and psychology.

Although limited in scope, this book will provide a wealth of information that will help any master level student in the pursuit of a career in counseling and psychology. It is the hope of the authors that graduate level students who are considering a masters degree in counseling and psychology will use this book as a resource when researching the appropriate field, necessary training, licensure requirements and best practices in different areas of counseling and psychology. The book also addresses the professional development of master level counselors by emphasizing the importance of training to work with diverse populations and the importance of following ethical practices and the pursuit of doctoral studies and counseling and psychology.

The book is divided into three sections. **Section One** is titled, Careers in Counseling and Psychology and includes information on pursuing careers in six different areas. *Chapter 1. Career Counseling as a Career Choice for Graduate Counselors* outlines the development of career counseling and provides information on the different arenas that career counselors are employed and the roles of responsibilities of career counselors in those arenas. *Chapter 2. Becoming a Transformed Professional School Counselor* gives a brief summary of the transformation of the new professional school counselor, provides the components of the new national model and the roles and responsibilities of school counselors at the elementary, middle and secondary levels. Finally the chapter provides certification requirements for all 50 states including the District of Columbia. *Chapter 3. Careers in Counseling at the Community College and University Level* list the different units that master level counselors are employed within colleges and universities. The chapter gives roles and responsibilities and competencies needed to function within those units. *Chapter 4. Careers in School Psychology* provides all the information needed to understand the roles, responsibilities and licensure and certification requirements of a school psychologist. *Chapter 5. Careers in Alcohol and Drug Counseling* provides a thorough description of the role of the addictions counselor, certification and licensing requirement, as well as competencies needed in this field. *Chapter 6. Careers in Corrections* outlines the counselor's role in the area of corrections, certification requirements, responsibilities and competencies needed to become an effective counselor in corrections.

Section Two Working with Families will introduce students to the role of a family and provide a sample of the structure of a Family Education Center. *Chapter 7. Working with families and couples as a Family Therapist* outlines the brief history of family therapy, provides information about working with today's family structures and methods of addressing issues that arise in families. The chapter also provides licensure and certification requirements. Chapter 8. *The Structure of a Family Education Center* gives an example of the structure of a family education center.

Section Three Counseling Competencies and Professional Development focuses on three areas of development. *Chapter 9. The importance of developing multicultural competencies in all settings* emphasizes the need to develop multicultural competencies when working in any setting, especially given the diversity that exists in society today. *Chapter 10. Exercising Legal and Ethical Practices* stresses the need to stay abreast of legal and ethical competencies in any field and need to protect oneself and the public.

Chapter 11. So you want to earn a doctorate: A personal account and advice for students interested in pursuing doctoral studies in counseling and psychology is an account of the experience of one professor's pursuit of a doctoral degree and outlines things students should consider with entertaining the notion of seeking advanced studies in counseling and psychology.

Section One

Careers in Counseling and Psychology

Career Counseling as a Career Choice for Graduate Counseling Students

1

By Karina M. Golden, Ph.D.

STUDENT AWARENESS OF CAREER COUNSELING AS A CAREER CHOICE

S tudents in graduate counseling programs often enter these programs without realizing the exciting career possibilities that are
available to them if they choose to become career counselors.
Many students enroll in counseling degree programs because they
know they want to help people and associate helping people with
providing personal or mental health counseling to clients. They are
often unaware that a career as a career counselor would provide them
with the opportunity to work with diverse populations in a rich array
of counseling settings where they can utilize creative delivery methods
to fulfill their desire to work as helping professionals (National Career
Development Association, 2000).

Career counseling may be especially attractive to students who aspire
to work as helping professionals but are not interested in focusing on
pathology. It emphasizes the importance of helping individuals to
make realistic career choices based on interests, skills, and abilities.
Career counselors use both traditional and non-traditional counseling
methods, including those such as: guided imagery and hypnosis. Career
counselors often encourage their clients to go beyond traditional jobs
and to seek the job of their dreams. Some of the career resources that
encourage this creative approach are books like *Do What You Love,
The Money Will Follow* (Sinetar, 1987); *The Live Your Dream Workbook*
(Chapman, 1994; *To Build the Life You Want, Create the Work You Love*

(Sinetar, 1995) and the career counseling classic *What Color Is Your Parachute* (Bolles, 2008). Becoming a career counselor could be a good choice for students who are goal-oriented and creative.

Many students become aware of career counseling as a professional career choice when they when take a required career counseling class as a part of their graduate studies. Graduate students are often surprised at the array of settings in which they can work as career counselors, such as schools, colleges, government agencies, and private industry. They are intrigued when they discover the diversity of the populations that need specialized services from career counselors, including minorities, persons with disabilities, immigrants, substance abusers, the mentally ill, returning women, and gay, lesbian, bisexual, and transgender clients. Entrepreneurial students may be inspired by the idea of owning their own business to work with these and other special populations.

Some students who enroll in graduate counseling and psychology programs have had prior exposure to the field of career counseling as career counseling clients themselves. They may have been inspired by having had a positive experience with a career counselor and are entering the field because of this positive interaction. Others may be interested in obtaining graduate training in the field of counseling because they are currently working in a job related to career counseling that does not require a degree and wish to develop their counseling skills to better serve their clients.

CAREER COUNSELING: A DIVERSE FIELD

The term "career counseling" is often used interchangeably with "career development," "vocational counseling," or "vocational guidance." Professionals who work in these fields are called "career counselors," "vocational counselors," or "vocational education counselors." The use of these different terms exists because the history of career counseling can be traced to the simultaneous growth of two different perspectives (Gladding, 1996; Herr and Cramer, 1999). The first is the career guidance movement, with its focus on vocational guidance, which has historically grown out of school and government interventions devised to provide individuals with vocational information and assist them in finding employment. The second is a more comprehensive career counseling approach. It is called the career development approach and it recognizes the importance of job placement but places additional emphasis on career development as a complex career counseling intervention. This approach assists individuals with occupational choice, including the role of values, identity, interests, abilities, and decision making skills. The career development approach acknowledges that career choice is not a one time decision but a series of decisions across the lifespan (Herr and Cramer, 1999).

Although career counselors focus their interventions on assisting clients with career development issues, the distinction between career and personal counseling is not always clear. The literature shows increasing support for the idea that career counseling and personal counseling are closely intertwined (Blustein, 1987; Brown, 1985; Nagel, Hoffman, and Hill, 1995). A position paper written jointly by the Association for Counselor Education and Supervision and the National Career Development Association underscores this premise (National Career Development Association, 2000). For while the initial focus of the intervention in career counseling is usually to assist a client with career issues, sometimes these issues cannot easily be separated from those that may arise during personal counseling. Career issues can have an effect on the mental health of the client, for a person who is unhappy with his or her work may exhibit signs of being depressed or anxious. This perspective suggests that successful career counselors must be prepared to recognize the importance of incorporating personal counseling skills as a part of the career counseling process. For example, a person who has been laid off from work not only needs assistance with finding a new job, but with negotiating the often confusing emotional reaction to this job loss which has been likened to the Kubler-Ross stages of death and dying: denial, anger, bargaining, depression, and acceptance (Borgen and Amundsen in Herr and Kramer, 1996, p. 96). In this instance, the task of the career counselor is to assist the client with his or her job search while acknowledging the need to provide personal helping skills to assist the client in healing from the emotional devastation that may arise as a result of job loss.

Career counselors may therefore incorporate personal counseling in their work to varying degrees depending on the setting in which they work and their personal comfort with working with these issues. Even if they choose not to address these issues in their practice, they need to be trained to recognize the need for this type of intervention so appropriate referrals can be made.

CAREER DEVELOPMENT THEORIES

Career counselors may emphasize one theoretical orientation in their work, but they are generally eclectic in their approach and may employ both traditional counseling theories and those career counseling theories which have evolved out of a deeper understanding of career development. Career counseling has moved beyond its initial role in its early years of providing career information to match people with jobs, to today's understanding of career development as a more complex process involving the role of self-concept, decision-making, and development across the lifespan (Andersen & Vandehey, 1999).

One of the earliest approaches to career counseling is the trait and factor approach introduced by Frank Parsons in 1909 which matches an individual's talents with the characteristics of a job (Herr and Cramer, 1996). One of the most well-known applications of this approach is John Holland's theory which links six personality types with six work environments and suggests that people are more satisfied with their work when their personality traits and the characteristics of their workplace are congruent (Holland, 1973). The psychodynamic approach focuses on career choice as the fulfillment of unconscious wishes. Roe (1957) has developed this concept and places special emphasis on the influences of early parenting and child rearing in shaping career choice. Developmental theories like those of Ginzberg (1972) and Super (1990) focus on career development across the lifespan. They suggest different stages of career development as a process of stages that unfold across a lifetime. Cognitive and behavioral approaches such as those proposed by Tiedemann and O'Hara (1963) which focuses on decision-making across seven stages of development and by Knefelkamp and Slepitza (1976) which emphasizes a hierarchal structure of career decision-making in college students may also be utilized. These are just some of the career counseling theories that can be integrated when conducting career counseling.

Career counselors may also incorporate traditional counseling theories to explain the motivation for career choice and to provide assistance with career development. Those who work from a psychoanalytic approach may incorporate a Freudian perspective may view career choice as the satisfaction of unconscious needs (Gladding, 1999). A Jungian perspective would also look at unconscious motives but is also likely to utilize the concept of the archetypes as well as Jungian personality theory as expressed through the Myers-Briggs Type Indicator (Myers & McCauley, 1985). An Adlerian approach would look at the role of birth order and may explore the client's feelings of inferiority and need for social interest (Herr and Cramer, 1996). A Rogerian person-centered approach would emphasize the importance of the career counselor's providing empathy, congruence, and positive regard to help facilitate the client's ability to make appropriate career choices. An existential therapist would encourage the client to recognize that he or she has both ultimate freedom and responsibility for career choices. The behavioral therapist would focus on getting clients to adapt healthy behaviors that would facilitate career choice and the cognitive behaviorist would emphasize the importance of recognizing thought patterns that can help or hinder career development (Gladding, 1996). In essence, any of the personal counseling theories can be employed to assist client's with their career development.

SKILLS NEEDED BY CAREER COUNSELORS

The paper *Preparing Counselors for a New Millennium* (National Career Development Association, 2000) argues that career counselors must possess a multitude of skills in order to deliver services effectively in a global economy. They must have an awareness of career counseling theories and demonstrate good helping skills. Career counselors must be familiar with ways of accessing local and global job trends. They must also be aware of career counseling resources, both print and non-print, to assist clients in understanding occupational choices. These include traditional sources like the *Occupational Outlook Handbook* published by the Bureau pf Labors Statistics (2009–2009) and O*net, as well as more frequently updated sources available on the internet. Career counselors must be familiar with career counseling assessments, including computerized assessments such as DISCOVER and computer assisted guidance systems. They must also be aware of best practices when using and interpreting assessments. Career counselors must be able to help clients with short and long-term career planning. In addition to working with individuals, many career counselors teach workshops and conduct career counseling groups. This means they must be trained in group counseling processes and educational delivery systems. This paper suggests that career counselors also need to pay attention to the spiritual dimension of career counseling as the choice of a career may be a spiritual process of finding one's life purpose or avocation and not just locating a job.

Since the role of the career counselor is so diverse, there have been many attempts to identify essential skills and objectives for the effective career counselor. *The Career Counselor's Handbook* (Figler and Bowles, 1999, p. 38) identifies twelve key skills of the career counselor: clarifying content, reflecting feeling, open-ended questioning, skill identifying, value clarifying, creative imaging, information giving, role-playing, spot-checking, summarizing, task setting, and establishing the Yes, Buts. They have also identified six objectives of career counseling: helping clients assume responsibility, imagine career ideas, use one's favorite functional and adaptive skills, deal with negative emotions, know how to determine steps to a career goal, and choose work that has meaning and purpose (Figler and Bowles, 1999, pp. 25–30).

The National Career Development Association (www.ncda.org) has defined twelve competencies to effectively facilitate career development. The Career Development Competencies as defined by the National Career Development's Career Development Facilitator curriculum (National Career Development Association, n.d.) include the following: helping skills, labor market information and resources, assessment, diverse populations, ethical and legal issues, career development models, employability skills, training clients and peers, program management/ implementation, promotions and public reform, technology, and consultation.

SPECIAL POPULATIONS AND SETTINGS FOR CAREER COUNSELORS

Career counselors may work in a variety of settings including schools, colleges, the government, private industry, and private practice. In their work they may address the needs of many special populations, including African Americans, Hispanics, Asians, and Native Americans. Career counselors, like all counselors, should therefore have training in working with diverse populations (Atkinson, 2004) and must be especially sensitive to their career differing counseling needs (Herr and Cramer, 1999). They should also be trained to work with these diverse populations at different ages and stages in different settings across the lifespan: individuals of elementary, middle and high school ages; college students of all ages; and early adulthood to post-retirement ages.

CAREER COUNSELING IN THE SCHOOLS

Some career counselors work with students in school settings whereas others may work with them at government, community based, or private practice settings. Career counselors agree that elementary school students would benefit from early interventions which would introduce them to careers, help them understand their strengths and weaknesses, break down stereotypes, and provide valuable role models (Gladding,

1999; Herr and Cramer, 1996). Middle school students would also benefit from these interventions plus more targeted interventions that would help students to identify appropriate careers, and understand the educational requirements and earning potentials of different careers. Additionally high school students need to learn resume writing, interviewing, and job search skills. These services are often provided by both school counselors and career counselors.

CAREER COUNSELORS IN COLLEGES AND UNIVERSITIES

Career counselors are also needed at the college level to assist undergraduate and graduate students of all ages. Career counselors often work in college or university career centers and provide career counseling, conduct career workshops, and hold job fairs. Career counselors assist students in understanding the marketability of their college majors and master's degrees and provide them with assistance in resume writing, interviewing skills, and job search skills (Gladding, 1999; Herr and Cramer, 1996). They also assist them in identifying further educational training that might be needed for certain professions.

CAREER COUNSELING WITH ADULTS

Adults are in need of career counseling at different points during their lifetimes (Herr and Cramer, 1996). In the early years adults may need counseling to develop a sense of career direction. Later adults need assistance with mid-life career changes. Employees who are in the workforce often have to cope with the need for additional training in order to further their careers. They need guidance to assist them in choosing appropriate training programs and to understand the implications of these choices. Individuals who are laid off or unemployed often need help in finding appropriate training or work where they can use their experience and transferable skills for new positions. Older workers often need assistance with career planning as they retire from their careers. Many older workers need assistance in creating post-retirement careers.

OTHER CAREER COUNSELING SETTINGS

Career counselors may also work in private business or in government or community settings. In these settings they respond to the needs of their clients according to the parameters defined by their place of work. They may assist persons in finding appropriate training, coping with unemployment, locating jobs, or changing careers.

Those who work in private practice may tailor their services to work with special populations such as adolescents, women, minorities, retirees or executives. They have the most freedom in their work style and work hours and may also deliver services to the community such as workshops and seminars.

CERTIFICATION AND TRAINING

Master's degree trained career counselors typically have degrees in counseling psychology, mental health counseling, career counseling, community counseling, and related fields. These degrees are usually offered through college or university counseling, education, or psychology divisions. Most of these degree programs identify themselves with the counseling profession by affiliating with the American Counseling Association (ACA). ACA is the professional organization for professional counselors. ACA acknowledges the importance of career counseling as a competency area for all counselors.

ACA has two professional divisions associated with career counseling, The National Career Development Association (NCDA) and the National Employment Counselors Association (NECA). Each of these associations has opportunities for representation at the state level. Members of these associations include professionals in business and industry, rehabilitation, government, private practice and education. They each publish a professional journal and set standards for best practices as career counselors.

The Council for the Accreditation of Counseling and Accredited Programs (CACREP) provides guidelines for certification of counselor education programs. Although not all counseling programs are

CACREP accredited, most voluntarily choose to follow the CACREP academic guidelines which identify eight core counseling areas: human growth and development, social and cultural diversity, relationships, group work, career development, assessment, research and program evaluation, and professional identity. Graduates of counseling programs who become career counselors therefore usually have training in these areas.

Educational attainment in these content areas is the basis for eligibility for national certification as a National Certified Counselor (NCC). This certification is granted through the National Board for Certified Counselors (NBCC) (www.nbcc.org). The test used to qualify for NBCC certification requires competency in career counseling. This test is used by many states for the testing portion of the requirements for state licensure in the states where licensure is required. Although requirements vary from state to state, most require the completion of 48 to 60 hours of course work in the eight designated content areas, the passing of an exam, and supervision by a mental health professional beyond the masters' degree. Individual state requirements can be viewed at the ACA website or by contacting the state's department of mental health licensing board. The requirements to be certified or licensed to practice career counseling and to administer and interpret career assessments also vary from state to state. Some career counselors who have master's degrees in counseling opt to become licensed as licensed professional counselors in their state. Many career counselors, however, are able to provide career counseling without state licensure or certification.

Students who graduate from a CACREP accredited program or a graduate program which follows CACREP guidelines will be required to take at least one three credit course in career counseling. Some graduate programs offer degrees in career counseling or specializations or certificates where students can enhance their career counseling skills by taking additional career counseling coursework or receiving additional supervision in this area. Students may also further their training in career counseling by choosing practicum and internship experiences in career counseling settings. They may also choose to receive post graduate supervision in this area. Many students graduate with a counseling degree and then receive on the job training as a career counselor.

CAREER DEVELOPMENT FACILITATORS

In recognition of the fact that career counseling consists of both persons with master's degree training in counseling and those who work in the profession without this training, the National Career Development Association (NCDA) developed the specialized certification of Career Development Facilitator (CDF). This certification is designed to provide training in career counseling competencies, especially for those who do not have master's degree training. The training provides coursework in career counseling areas identified by NCDA as being essential for the delivery of effective career counseling services. This optional training is nationally recognized and may be an optional certification for counselors working as career counselors.

NEED FOR CAREER COUNSELORS

The need for career counselors is growing as the world of work becomes more complex. Job seekers are often bewildered by the thousands of jobs that are available to them and the continual changes in requirements and training for these jobs. Additionally, as more people reach retirement age they are finding that they need to supplement their incomes with additional income. This population is seeking career counseling to assist them in finding career direction. The Department of Labor's reference The Occupational Outlook Handbook, 2008–2009 edition (www.bls.gov/oco/ocos067.htm) uses the terms career and vocational counseling interchangeably under the general heading of counselors. It suggests that educational, vocational, and school counselors work in the schools by providing occupational information and sometimes by running centers and career education programs. It further reports that the majority of career and vocational counselors work outside the school setting and are involved in helping individuals with career decisions. Vocational counselors explore and evaluate the client's education, training, work history, interests, skills, and personality traits. They also arrange for aptitude and achievement tests to help the client make career decisions. They also work with individuals to develop job-search skills and assist clients in locating and applying for jobs. In addition, career counselors provide support to persons experiencing job loss, job stress, or other career transitions (Bureau of Labor Statistics, 2008–2009).

Since this source combines career and vocational counselors with educational and other kinds of counselors, the exact figures for those working as career counselors are unclear. However, according to this resource, the need for counselors is expected to be above average. Salaries for educational, vocational, and school counselors in May 2006 were $47,530. Those who work in private industry may have higher salaries. The salary for career counselors who have well-established private practices may also be higher. Career counselors often supplement their incomes by doing additional workshops or consulting.

FOR FURTHER INFORMATION, CONTACT:

American Counseling Association, 5999 Stevenson Avenue, Alexandria, Virginia 22304. www.counseling.org

Council for Accreditation of Counseling and Related Education al Programs, American Counseling Association, 5999 Stevenson Avenue, Alexandria, Virginia 22304. www.cacrep.org

National Board of Certified Counselors, Inc., 3 Terrace way, Suite D, Greensboro, North Carolina, www.nbcc.org

National Career Development Association www.ncda.org

National Employment Counselors Association www.neca.org

REFERENCES

Andersen, P. & Vandehey, M. (1999). *Career counseling and development in a global economy*. New York: Lhaska Press.

Atkinson, D. R. (2004). Counseling American minorities. New York: McGraw Hill.

Blustein, D. L. (1987). Integrating career counseling and psychotherapy: A comprehensive treatment strategy. *Psychotherapy*, 24, 794–799.

Bowles, R. N. (2008). *What color is your parachute?* Berkeley, CA: Ten Speed Press.

Brown, D. (1985). Career counseling: before, after, or instead of personal counseling. *Vocational Guidance Quarterly*, 33, 197–201.

Bureau of Labor Statistics, U.S> Department of Labor. *Occupational Outlook Handbook, 2008–2009 edition*. Retrieved from http:/www.bls.gov/oco/ocos067htm on May 8, 2009.

Chapman, J. (1994). *The live your dream workbook*. Van Nuys, CA.: Newcastle Publishing Company.

Figler, H. & Bowles, R.N. (1999). *The career counselor's handbook*. Berkely, Ca.: Ten Speed Press.

Ginzberg (1972). Toward a theory of occupational choice: A restatement. *Vocational Guidance Quarterly*, 20, 169–176.

Gladding, S. (1996). *Counseling: A comprehensive profession*. Third ed. Englewood Cliffs, N.J.: Prentice Hall.

Herr, E. L. (1989). Career development and mental health. *Journal of Career development*, 16, 5–18.

Herr, E. L. and Cramer, S. H. (1999). *Career counseling and guidance through the lifespan*. New York: Longman publishers.

Holland, J. L. (1973). *Making vocational choices. A theory of careers*. Englewood Cliffs, N. J.: Prentice Hall.

Knefelkamp, L.L. & Slepitza, R. (1976). A cognitive developmental model of career development—An adaptation of Perry's scheme. *Counseling Psychologist*, 6, 53–58.

Nagel, D.P., Hoffman, M.A. & Hill, C. E. (1995). A comparison of verbal response modes used by master's level career counselors and other helpers. *Journal of Counseling and Development*, 74, 101–104.

National Career Development Association. Career Development Competencies. Retrieved from: http://associationdatabase.com/aws/NCDA/pt/sp/facilitator-overview-competencies on May 12, 2009.

National Career Development Association. (2000). *Preparing counselors for career development in the new millennium. ACES/NCDA position paper. December, 2000. Retrieved from www.ncda.org on May 6, 2009.*

Niles, S. G. & Harris-Bowlsbey (2002). *Career development interventions in the 21ˢᵗ century.* Upper Saddle River, N.J.: Merrill Prentice Hall.

Roe A. (1956). *The psychology of occupations.* New York: Wiley.

Sinetar, M. (1987). *Do what you love, the money will follow.* New York: Dell.

Sinetar, M. (1995). *To build the life you want, create the work you love.* New York: St. Griffith's.

Super, D.E. (1990). A life-span, life-development approach to career development. In D. Brown & L. Brooks (Eds). *Career choice and development: Applying contemporary theories to practice* (pp. 197–261). San Francisco: Jossey Bass.

Becoming the New "Transformed" Professional School Counselor

2

By Audrey A. Lucas, Ph.D.

INTRODUCTION

Children and adolescents today face many challenges that threaten their academic success and overall development. Therefore, a decision to become a professional school counselor is a noble decision. In addition to the learning challenges some children must overcome, the incidences of violence in the schools have increased. According to Haberman (2008), approximately 525,000 attacks, shakedowns, and robberies occur in secondary schools in one month. Three million incidents of assault, rape, robbery, and thefts occur on school properties annually. School counselors today face many issues such as: bullying, weapons, a decline in parent involvement, peer pressure, teenage pregnancy and other problems that affect student achievement. However many studies have shown how effective school counselors have been supporting academic achievement (Sink & Stroh, 2003; Cook & Kaffenberger, 2003; Lee, 1993; Boutwell & Myrick, 1992; Holcomb-McCoy, 2007; Sink, 2008), promoting social skills development (Verduyn, Lord & Forrest, 1990) dealing with family issues (Rose & Rose, 1992; Omizo and Omizo, 1998; Bryan & Henry, 2008,) and assisting students with gaining access to resources in the community (Canfield, Ballard, Osmon & McCune, 2004; Schaefer-Schiumo & Ginsberg, 2003; Hermann & Finn, 2002). So the school counselor's role in the school is vital to student success. This chapter will discuss the job of the new transformed school counselor by providing a brief history of the profession, give a description of roles and responsibilities at the elementary, middle, and high school levels and provide a listing of school counselor certification requirements from all 50 states and the District of Columbia.

EVOLUTION OF THE TRANSFORMED SCHOOL COUNSELOR

Although initially the development of children was viewed as a family responsibility, societal changes began to dictate the necessity for programs and personnel in the schools to play a more active role in supporting that development. (Dollarhide & Saginak, 2008). The school counseling profession can be traced back to the early 1900s. One of the first counselor type activities was initiated by Jesse B. Davis, a high school principal, who instructed his teachers to use journal writing in their English classes to address character, behavior and career development. In 1908 Frank Parsons, "the father of guidance" in his work with the Boston Vocation Bureau, coined the term, "vocational guidance." Parsons was active in the development of the Boston Vocation Bureau which helped outline a system of vocational guidance in the Boston public schools. According to stateuniversity.com(2003), the work of the bureau influenced the need for and the use of vocational guidance both in the United States and other countries. By 1918, there were documented accounts of the bureau's influence as far away as Uruguay and China. In 1913 the National Vocational Guidance Association was formed and it helped to legitimize school counseling programs and increase the number of guidance counselors in this country and by 1918, more than 900 high schools had some type of vocational guidance system.

As the result of the Industrial Revolution, the influx of young people into the workforce, the need to produce a better workforce, ills in society and economic changes the need arose for school counselors to focus on more than guidance and vocational choice (Gysbers, 2001). School counselors began to provide services to students that were more directed toward the total development of students in order to assist them with handling the new demands of society. However, during the time of the Great Depression in the 1930s, guidance programs began to suffer. It wasn't until the George Dean Act of 1938 which provided funds for guidance programs, did guidance programs began to pick up. From the 1940s through the 1950s several theoretical approaches emerged and gave way to a more didactic school counselor (Gysbers, 2001). C. Gilbert Wrenn, in his 1962 book, The Counselor in a Changing World, brought to light the need for more cultural sensitivity on the part of school counselors, developmental theories such as Frederick Perl's gestalt therapy, William Glasser's reality therapy, Abraham Maslow and Rollo May's existential approach, and John Krumboltz's behavioral counseling approach provided several techniques for school counselors to use in addressing children (http://education.stateuniversity.com.).

As the profession continued to evolve, by the 1970's the emphasis on the school counseling profession was that of accountability. School counselors, as well as educators, were called upon to demonstrate program effectiveness; so program evaluation became an important component of the school counseling program. It became apparent that not all programs were effective, there were differences in the way programs were structured and there was no comprehensive school counseling model. In 1971, the University of Missouri-Columbia was awarded a grant by the Office of Education and under the direction of Norman C. Gysbers, who has been identified by some as modern contributor to the transformation of the school counselor, was asked to assist each state, the District of Columbia, and Puerto Rico in developing models or guides for implementing career guidance and counseling and placement programs in their local schools. Their work resulted in the first framework for a model for school counselor programs. This new comprehensive guidance program model contained three interrelated categories, curriculum based, individual of functions and on-call functions (Gybers & Henderson, 2001).

This was a major occurrence for the school counseling profession. The next major occurrence was the development of the school counselor standards by the American School Counseling Association, "ASCA." As a part of the standards, ASCA recognized the school counselor's switch from taking a reactive approach to a proactive and preventive approach to providing services in the schools. In the publication "Sharing the Vision: The National Standards for School Counseling Programs," ASCA stated that:

"School counseling programs are developmental by design, focusing on the needs, interests, and issues related to the various stages of student growth. There is a commitment to individual differences and the maximum development of human potential.

The School Counselor is a certified mental health professional who assists students, parents, and administrators using three helping processes:

1. Counseling is a complex helping process in which the counselor establishes a trusting and confidential relationship with individuals and groups focusing on problem solving, decision making, and personal issues related to psychological, social, and educational development.
2. Consultation is a cooperative process in which the counselor assists others to think through problems and to develop skills that makes them more effective in working with students.
3. Coordination is a leadership process in which the school counselor helps to organize and manage a school's counseling process.

ASCA identified five interventions: individual counseling, small group counseling, large group counseling, consultation and coordination. The next transformation occurred in 1997, when DeWitt Wallace-Reader's Digest Fund and The Education Trust developed a national agenda which focused on examining school counseling programs by looking at school counseling preparation. Their study found that many school counseling preparation programs had different methods of training and some provided generic counseling and psychology courses that were not specific to school settings. As a result, the Education Trust, with the support of DeWitt Wallace funds, created grants with the purpose of transforming school counselor preparation programs. Several Universities took part in the study and the information gained provided the framework for training the new school counselor. These changes occurred during the time of "school reform" which meant school counselors, as well as all professionals who had a role in the schools, needed to join the reformation movement. So in response, the American School Counseling Association created the National Model for School Counseling Programs. Although the national model was never intended to be a blueprint, it provided a framework for future school counseling programs. In support of the new transforming school counseling in 2003, the Education Trust and Met Life Foundation created The National Center for Transforming School Counseling, which was a collaborative effort between schools, state departments of education, school counselor professional associations, institutions of higher education and school districts across the country (http://www2.edtrust.org.). As a result of the initiative, the transformed school counselor's roles shifted from the three "C's," collaboration, counseling and consultation to advocacy, leadership, teaming, collaboration, counseling, consultation, and data driven.

From the University of Missouri-Columbia and Norman C. Gysbers' creation of Comprehensive Guidance Program Model, to ASCA's national standards and the National Framework for School Counseling Programs, researchers have been emphasizing the need for school counseling programs to provide the most comprehensive school counseling programs. Other researchers have continued to contribute to the transformation. For example, Cheryl Holcomb McCoy emphasized need for social justice focused school counseling programs. In Holcomb McCoy's (2007) book titled, "School Counseling to Close the Achievement Gap: A social justice framework for success," she outlines the importance of understanding the impact of ethnicity on identity formation and academic performance. Holcomb McCoy (2007) discusses the roles, power and multicultural competencies of school counselors and emphasizes the importance of developing a social justice focused school counseling program that assesses the counselor's skills and beliefs, the student's needs, and the importance of accountability and the use of data. The new transformed school counselor has evolved into an advocate, coordinator, collaborator and leader in the schools. Transformed school counselors are more proactive and accountable, they understand diversity and the need for multicultural competencies and social justice and the transformed school counselor realize the futility of the use of data.

ASCA'S NATIONAL MODEL FOR SCHOOL COUNSELING PROGRAMS

ASCA's National Model includes four components, the Foundation, Delivery System, Management System and Accountability and includes four themes, Leadership, Advocacy, Collaboration and Teaming and Systemic Change. The Foundation includes the beliefs and philosophy of the program and explains what the program will do. The Delivery system outlines how the program will be implemented. It provides a framework from which activities can be delivered, which include guidance curriculum, individual student planning, responsive services and systems support. The Management system outlines how the program is managed, by whom it is managed and based on what information is it managed. The Management system includes management agreements, an advisory council, use of data, action plans and use of time. The Accountability system is the method by which the counselors communicate the results of the activities and the effects those activities have on student development, specifically student achievement. The Accountability system includes results reports, performance standards and program audits.

ELEMENTARY SCHOOLS

In the Guide to State Laws and Regulations on Professional School Counseling, the American Counseling Association Office of Public Policy and Legislation stated:

"School Counseling Programs are developmental by design, focusing on needs, interests and issues related to the various stages of student growth. There are objectives, activities, special services and expected outcomes, with an emphasis on helping students to learn more effectively and efficiently. There is a commitment to individual uniqueness and the maximum development of human potential."

Below is a brief description of the unique developmental changes of students and a list of activities recommended for delivery of responsive services at the elementary, middle and secondary levels.

Developmentally elementary school children have many social, emotional and physical needs. School counselors play an integral role in nurturing a child's total development. Eric Erikson's psychosocial stages of development describe certain developmental tasks that children in elementary school must learn to successfully navigate. From the pre-school ages of 3 to 5, Erikson (1990) characterizes this developmental stage as the "exploration stage." It is at this stage when children need to begin asserting control and power over their environment. Success at this stage leads to a sense of purpose. Children who try to exert too much power experience disapproval, resulting in a sense of guilt. At ages 6 to 11 years old, Erikson characterizes this developmental stage as the school age stage of 'industry vs. inferiority' when children need to cope with new social and academic demands. Success at this stage leads to a sense of competence, while failure results in feelings of inferiority. School counselors must consider the needs of children at each stage of development, while providing academic support, promoting healthy social skills and assisting with emotional regulation. Below is a list of the activities listed in the national model's delivery system for school counselors to use when working with elementary school children.

School Guidance Curriculum
1. Academic support, including organizational, study and test taking skills
2. Goal setting and decision-making
3. Career awareness, exploration and planning
4. Education on understanding self and others

5. Peer relationships, coping strategies and effective social skills
6. Communication, problem-solving and conflict resolution
7. Substance abuse education 8. Multicultural/diversity awareness

Individual Student Planning
1. Academic planning
2. Goal setting/decision- making
3. Education on understanding of self, including strengths and weaknesses
4. Transition plans

Responsive Services
1. Individual and small-group counseling
2. Individual/family/school crisis intervention
3. Conflict resolution
4. Consultation/collaboration
5. Referrals

System Support
1. Professional development
2. Consultation, collaboration and teaming
3. Program management and operation

Middle and Secondary School

During the passage from childhood to adolescence, according to ASCA (2007), middle school students are characterized by: a need to explore a variety of interests; connecting their learning in the class-room to its practical application in life and work; high levels of activity coupled with frequent fatigue due to rapid growth; a search for their own unique identity as they begin turning more frequently to peers rather than parents for ideas and affirmation; extreme sensitivity to the comments from others; and heavy reliance on friends to provide comfort, understanding and approval. Secondary school is viewed the final transition into adulthood and the world of work as students begin separating from parents and exploring and defining their independence. Students are deciding who they are, what they do well, and what they will do when they graduate (ASCA, 2007) Throughout the adolescent years, students are evaluating their strengths, skills and abilities and their biggest influence is their peer group. They are searching for a place to belong and they rely on peer acceptance and feedback. They face increased pressures regarding risk taking behaviors involving sex, alcohol and drugs, while exploring the boundaries of more acceptable behavior and mature, meaningful relationships. They need guidance in making concrete and compounded decisions. They must deal with academic pressures as they face high-stakes testing, the challenges of college admissions, the scholarship and financial aid application process and entrance into a competitive job market (ASCA, 2007).

From the ages 13–18, this development stage is characterized by a time when the adolescent asks, "Who am I?" as adolescents begin to form their identity. Erickson (1990) contends that when identity formation is not accomplished, adolescents experience "role confusion." Erickson (1990) called this stage one of "storm and stress." Success during this stage leads to self acceptance and self confidence. Below is a list of activities suggested by national models within the delivery system that school counselors can use when assisting middle and secondary students with achieving academic success, self-confidence and preparing for transition to adulthood.

MIDDLE SCHOOL
School Guidance Curriculum
1. Academic skills support
2. Organizational, study and test-taking skills
3. Education in understanding self and others

4. Coping strategies
5. Peer relationships and effective social skills
6. Communication, problem-solving, decision-making and conflict resolution
7. Career awareness, exploration and planning
8. Substance abuse education
9. Multicultural/diversity awareness

Individual Student Planning
1. Goal-setting/decision- making
2. Academic planning
3. Career planning
4. Education in understanding of self, including strengths and weaknesses
5. Transition planning

Responsive Services
1. Individual and small group counseling
2. Individual/family/school crisis intervention
3. Peer facilitation
4. Consultation/collaboration
5. Referrals

System Support
1. Professional development
2. Consultation, collaboration and teaming
3. Program management and operation

Secondary School

Classroom Guidance

1. Academic skills support
2. Organizational, study and test-taking skills
3. Post-secondary planning and application process
4. Career planning
5. Education in understanding self and others
6. Coping strategies
7. Peer relationships and effective social skills
8. Communication, problem-solving, decision-making, conflict resolution and study skills
9. Career awareness and the world of work
10. Substance abuse education
11. Multicultural/diversity awareness

Individual Student Planning

1. Goal setting
2. Academic plans
3. Career plans
4. Problem solving
5. Education in understanding of self, including strengths and weaknesses
6. Transition plans

Responsive Services

1. Individual and small-group counseling
2. Individual/family/school crisis intervention
3. Peer facilitation
4. Consultation/collaboration
5. Referrals

System Support

1. Professional development
2. Consultation, collaboration and teaming
3. Program management and operation (ASCA, 2005)

CERTIFICATION, LICENSURE, OR ENDORSEMENT

Below are the credentialing requirements for school counselors. According to Lum (2002), credentials can be called "certification," "licensure" or "endorsements." State University.com (2003) identifies the following requirements for the credentialing of professional school counselors.

1. All states and the District of Columbia require a graduate education (i.e., completion of some graduate-level course work), with forty-five states and the District of Columbia requiring a master's degree in counseling and guidance or a related field.
2. Majority of states also require that graduate work include a certain number of practicum hours, ranging from 200 to 700, in a school setting.
3. Majority of states require applicants to have previous teaching experience. Some of these states allow students to gain experience through the graduate program by means of internships.
4. About half of the states require standardized testing as part of the credentialing process. Many of these tests simply cover basic mathematics, writing, and reading skills, while some states require more specialized tests covering the field of guidance and counseling. Some states require a minimum number of course credit hours specifically related to guidance and counseling; others require students to take courses in other subject areas, such as education of children with disabilities, multicultural issues, substance abuse, state and federal laws and constitutions, applied technology, and identification and reporting of child abuse.

5. Most states recognize credentials from other states and most states require applicants to undergo a criminal background check. (http://education.stateuniversity.com)

CERTIFICATION REQUIREMENTS BY STATE

In addition to the general requirements, each state has its own credentialing requirements. The information below comes from the American School Counseling Associations (http://www.schoolcounselor.org/). Because certification requirements are frequently revised, it is important to review state certification requirements regularly.

State	Examination	Teaching Experience required	Reciprocity
Alabama	Praxis	Yes	NCATE only
Alaska			Yes
Arkansas	Praxis		Yes
California			Yes
Colorado	PACE or experience		Yes
Connecticut	Praxis or 1000 on SAT	Yes or Experience	No
Delaware	Praxis	Yes or 1 yr Internship	Yes
Dist. of Columbia	Praxis	Yes	Yes
Florida	CLAST		Yes w/valid current certification
Georgia	GACE		Yes
Hawaii	Praxis		Yes
Illinois	ISBE		Yes with 2 yrs experience

State	Examination	Teaching Experience required	Reciprocity
Indiana			Yes with conditions
Iowa			Yes
Kansas	Praxis		Yes
Kentucky		Yes or 2 yrs Experience	Yes
Louisiana	NTE	Yes	No
Maine	Praxis		Yes
Maryland			Yes
Massachusetts	State exam		Yes
Michigan	State exam		Yes
Minnesota			No
Mississippi	Praxis		Yes
Missouri			Yes
Montana			Yes
Nebraska	Praxis or CMEEBST	2 yrs.	No
Nevada			NASDTEC members
New Hampshire			NHDOE approved program
New Jersey			Yes
New Mexico	State Exam		No
New York			Yes
North Carolina			Yes with specific states
North Dakota		Yes	No
Ohio	NTE or Praxis		Yes
Oregon	Praxis		Yes
Pennsylvania	Praxis		No

State	Examination	Teaching Experience required	Reciprocity
Rhode Island			Yes
South Carolina	Praxis		Yes
South Dakota			No
Tennessee	Praxis	Yes	Yes
Texas	State Exam	Yes	No
Utah			Yes
Vermont	Praxis		Yes
Virginia			Yes
Washington	University Comprehensive exam or NCE		Yes
Wisconsin			Yes specific states
Wyoming	Yes		Yes

Students interested in becoming a professional school counselor should consider the importance of working with students and how their work may provide the only support some students will get as they seek to reach their true academic potential. It is a very important profession and the preparation should be taken seriously. ASCA has outlined a school counseling program framework and many have worked to transform the school counselor's role in the school and to make sure the school counselor is a vital force in school reform. States have determined the backgrounds needed to be an effective certified school counselor. Graduate students interested in this profession should adhere to following the requirements and preparation with commitment and hard work. The rewards of this profession will outweigh any sacrifices a graduate student will make to meet the certification requirements.

REFERENCES

American School Counselor Association/Hatch, T. & Bowers, J. (2005). *The ASCA National Model: A framework for school counseling programs, (2nd ed.)* Alexandria, VA: Author.

Brigman, G., & Campbell, C. (2003). Helping students improve academic achievement and school success behavior. *Professional School Counseling, 7,* 91–98.

Campbell, C.A. and Dahir, C.A. 1997. Sharing the vision: the national standards for school counseling programs.

Dahir, C.A. and Stone, D.B. 2003. Accountability: A m.e.a.s.u.r.e. of the impact school counselors have on student achievement. *Professional School Counseling,* Vol. 6, N. 3.

Dollarhide, C.T and Saginak, K.A. (2008). *Comprehensive School Counseling Programs: K-12 Delivery systems in action.* Pearson, Boston, MA.

Dimmitt, C. 2003. Transforming School Counseling Practice through Collaboration and the Use of Data: A Study of Academic Failure in High School. *Professional School Counselor,* June 6:5.

Gysbers, N.C. 2001. School guidance and counseling in the 21st century: remember the past into the future. *Professional School Counseling,* Dec 2001.

Gysbers, N.C. 2004. Comprehensive guidance and counseling programs: the evolution of accountability. *Professional School Counseling,* Vol. 8, No. 1.

Gysbers, N.C. & Henderson, P. (2000). *Developing and managing your school guidance program.* Alexandria VA: American Counseling Association.

Holcomb-McCoy, C. (2007). *School counseling to close the achievement gap: A social justice framework for success.* Thousand Oaks, CA: Corwin Press.

Holcomb-McCoy, C. (2008). A response to "social privilege, social justice and group counseling: an inquiry. *Journal for Specialist in Group Work,* Vol. 33, No. 4.

Holcomb-McCoy, C. (2005). Ethnic identity development in early adolescence: implications and recommendations for middle school counselors. *Professional School Counseling,* Vol. 8, No. 5.

Lum, C. (2003). *A guide to state laws and regulations on professional school counseling.* American Counseling Association. Office of Public Policy & Legislation. Alexandria, VA.

Musheno, S. and Talbert, M. (2002). The transformed school counselor in action. *Theory Into Practice,* Vol. 41, No. 3.

Paisley, P.O. and Borders, D. (1995). School counseling: an evolving specialty. *Journal of Counseling & Development*, Vol. 74, N. 2.

Popham, W.J. (1995). *New assessment methods for school counselors.* ERIC Clearinghouse on Counseling and Student Services. Greensboro, NC.

Rowell, L. (2005). Collaborative action research and school counselors. *Professional School Counselor*, Vol. 9, No. 1.

Scarborough, J & Luke, M. (2008). School counselors walking the walk and talking the talk: a grounded theory of effective program implementation. *Professional School Counseling*, Vol. 11, n. 6.

Schafer, W.D. (1995). *Assessment skills for school counselor.* ERIC Clearinghouse on Assessment and Evaluation.

Schmidt, J.J. and Clechalski, J.C. (2001). School counseling standards: a summary and comparison with other student services' standards. *Professional School Counseling*, Vol. 4, No. 5.

Sink, C. (2008). School counselors and teachers: collaborations for higher student achievement. *Elementary School Journal.* Vol. 108, n. 5.

Ukpokodu, O. N. (2007). Preparing socially conscious teachers: a social justice-oriented teacher education, Multicultural Education, Vol. 15, No. 1.

Verduyn, C.M., Lord, W. & Forrest, G.C. 1990. Social skills training in schools: an evaluation study. *Journal of Adolescence*, Vol. 13.

Whiston, S.C. 2002. Response to the past, present and future of school counseling: raising some issues. Professional School Counseling.

American School Counseling Association, www.schoolcounselor.org.

http://www2.edtrust.org/EdTrust/Transforming+School+Counseling/main

Academic advisors/counselors must also have knowledge of retention issues and retention efforts at their institution. Because academic advisors/counselors have direct contact with students, many times they become aware of problems that impact a student's ability to be successful at the university. Academic advisors/counselors should be aware of the retention support available to students, such as opportunities to withdraw from classes, audits, tutoring, peer support and etc. Colleges and Universities are driven by retention and take retention seriously. Most have functioning committees which deal specifically with student retention. Academic advisors/counselors should participate on these committees to gain information needed to help students who are at risk for failing and to provide information to the committees from the knowledge they have gained while working with students.

CAREER AND COOPERATIVE EDUCATION

Colleges and universities also hire master level graduates to work in career and cooperative education units to assist students with professional development. Career counselors assist students and alumni who are in the process of identifying careers and majors that are suitable for their career goals and help those in acquiring skills and abilities needed to make informed decisions related to career planning (www.bowiestate.edu). Career counselors do this by assisting students in finding internship opportunities that promote professional development and job readiness. Internships create opportunities for students to work in the field they are interested in prior to committing to the education and training required in that field. Internships are also degree requirements for some academic programs. Many academic units work with the career center in finding appropriate internship opportunities for their students.

Career counselors also assist students with selecting professional programs. These counselors coordinate and administer professional testing programs such as the LSAT, GRE and MCAT. Career counselors often provide test preparation workshops and monitor special testing accommodations for students in need. Master level graduates are also hired to assist in providing cooperative education support. A cooperative education experience, commonly known as a "co-op," provides academic credit for structured job experience. Cooperative education assists in helping students make the school-to-work transition, participate in service learning, and experiential learning initiatives.

There are two types of co-op plans in used at some Universities:

- Parallel Co-op: A Parallel Co-op is like a part-time job. The student goes to school full-time and works about 20 hours per week each semester. Students receive six credits for Parallel Co-op.
- Alternating Co-op: With an Alternating Co-op, the student alternates semesters between full-time work and full-time study. Students receive 12 credits for Alternating Co-op.

Co-op counselors should always keep abreast of employment trends and skills necessary to support a variety of careers. They should establish job banks and host job fairs for students. It is imperative that they establish partnerships with the business community and within these partnerships assist businesses with employee recruitment.

ADMISSIONS AND RECRUITMENT OFFICES

Some college and universities hire master level graduates to serve in the areas of admissions and recruitment. Admissions counselors are responsible for recruitment, reviewing applications, and assisting with graduation clearance. As a recruiter, the counselors visit high schools and attend college fairs. Recruitment counselors must be aware of admissions requirements, articulation agreements, degree offerings, student activities and financial aid. Master level graduates also work as admission counselors. Responsibilities required of admissions counselors include reviewing applications and retrieving documents needed for admissions and working with prospective students by assisting them through the admission process. They streamline the admissions process by facilitating the first step in the review of applications. Academic departments have specific admission requirements for their programs and the admissions counselor is responsible for forwarding those applications that meet that criteria. Admissions counselors are responsible for reviewing transcripts from transfer students applying to the university. Many two year colleges have entered into articulation agreements with surrounding four year colleges, these agreements assist students with completing a two year program that supports the requirements of academic programs at the partner four year institutions.

Admissions counselors will need to have knowledge of "articulation agreements" that exists between colleges and universities. Admissions counselors must also be aware of accreditation bodies when reviewing transcripts for admissions into the university. For example, on the eastern region one of the accreditation organizations is the Middle States Association of Colleges and Schools. The Middle States Commission on Higher Education is the unit of the Middle States Association of Colleges and Schools that accredits degree-granting colleges and universities in the Middle States region, which includes Delaware, the District of Columbia, Maryland, New Jersey, New York, Pennsylvania, Puerto Rico, the U.S. Virgin Islands, and several locations internationally.

The Commission is a voluntary, non-governmental, membership association that defines, maintains, and promotes educational excellence across institutions with diverse missions, student populations, and resources. It examines each institution as a whole, rather than specific programs within institutions. (http://www.msche.org/). It is the mission of the organization is to provide a nongovernmental voluntary accreditation process that uses peer review and promotes public confidence in the services of colleges and universities. Admissions counselors must understand how important accreditation is and whether a transfer student gaining admissions is coming from an accredited school.

JOB DESCRIPTION FOR AN ADMISSIONS COUNSELOR
Position Announcement Ad
Title: Senior Admissions Officer

University's, Admissions office seeks a Senior Admissions Officer reporting to the Dean of Admissions. The individual will coordinate international recruitment, including developing and implementing recruitment strategies worldwide and travel in specific geographic regions. The individual will also work with international alumnae and international student volunteers on-campus. General admissions responsibilities will include promoting the College to prospective students and their families and interpreting the admissions policies and procedures, conducting interviews and information sessions, planning and coordinating high school outreach programs, and participating in application review and selection. At a minimum, a bachelor's degree from a liberal arts institution and previous experience in selective college or university admissions, educational advising or relevant experience, preferably 3 or more years are required. Master's degree strongly preferred. Excellent oral/written communication, highly developed organizational skills, ability to work independently and as part of a team, as well as computer literacy are also required. Knowledge of world educational systems as well as an understanding of the values of a liberal arts education for women and the ability to articulate these values effectively is essential. Must be willing to work extended hours and weekends at certain times of the year.

STUDENT AFFAIRS AND STUDENT DEVELOPMENT

Master level graduates also work in the areas of student affairs and student development. Counselors who work in the area of student development provides support to the entire student population, but are housed in many different units. Master level graduates who work in the area of student development usually provide services through the Student Affairs office and other non academic support service units. These counselors operate based on theories of student development and adapt the basic assumptions that:

- the individual student must be considered as a whole.
- each student is a unique person and must be treated as such.
- the total environment of the student is educational and must be used to help the student achieve full development.
- the major responsibility for a student's personal and social development rests with the student and his/her personal resources. (http://en.wikipedia.org/wiki/Student_development)

It is important that counselors who work in the are of student development be knowledgeable of the requirements for many different programs. For example, these counselors may be hired to oversee honors programs and assist students with the contact information, application processes and requirements for induction and selection into these programs. Counselors in the area of student development usually oversee and advise student organizations such as fraternities and sororities. Although many student organizations have national governing bodies, they exist on college campuses at the invitation of the University. Student development counselors may be required to provide university oversight of these organizations.

Counselors who work in the area of student development may also be required to provide support to special populations, like international students, veterans and disabled students. These services include processing visas, loans, providing and monitoring accommodations and providing counseling and academic support services to these specific student populations. These counselors must have knowledge of the regulations governing each of these student populations. For example, the American with Disabilities Act governs how institutions provide access to services for students with disabilities and the Association on Higher Education and Disabilities outlines best practices for students with disabilities; the office of Veterans Affairs governs the funding and support services provided to veterans and the Department of Immigration governs regulates the granting of visas to international students. Counselors working in the area of student development should promote holistic development and must have good interpersonal skills and knowledge of techniques used to encourage and empower students to succeed while addressing social development in addition to academic development.

MENTAL HEALTH COUNSELING

Master level counselors who are interested in providing therapeutic services and do not wish to work in private practices or K-12 schools, should consider working in a college counseling center. The American College Counselor Association, "ACCA" is the organization that brings together mental health professionals who provide counseling services at the college level. ACCA's (2008) president stated that:

> "College counseling is about the whole person. College mental health practitioners ... are all invested in student development and student success. With the increase in the severity of presenting concerns on college campuses today, we must all work together to provide excellent comprehensive services for our students."

Mental health counselors provide mental health support to students, faculty and staff. Types of services are usually dependent on the Counseling Center's mission, number and types of employees hired and the university population. Services can include assessment, career counseling, personal counseling and crises counseling. Services can be delivered in individual and group sessions. According to Schwarz (2006) college students today are seen by college counselors as being more disturbed than 1 to 3 years ago. For this reason, college counselors encounter may many psychological challenges that need to be addressed in order for students to be successful in college. For example, college athletes deal with problems around academic success such as, athletic success, physical health, multiple relationships and the loss of athletic scholarships (Houghton, 2001). It is important the mental health counselors at the college level is prepared to address a variety of populations, with ethnic differences, learning differences, communication barriers and physical and medical needs.

JOB DESCRIPTION IN A COUNSELING CENTER
Department of Counseling Services
Salary commensurate with qualifications/experience

Position Description This position provides personal counseling and program development primarily to residential students and athletes and is required to work day, evenings and weekends in concert with residential and athletic student's recreational schedules.

Responsibilities include, but are not limited to, the following: Provide personal counseling; short-term individual and group counseling; coordinate referrals of long-term clients to local community resources; provide crisis intervention and conflict resolution for students, faculty, and staff; and coordinate and develop programs and services as needed.

Minimum Qualifications

Master's degree in Counseling, Social Work or related field; at least two years directly related experience; and must meet eligibility requirements for professional licensure through the State of Wyoming Mental Health Professional Licensing Board.

Desired Qualifications

Master's degree in Counseling, Social Work or related field with an emphasis or experience in student personnel services or higher education; counseling skills in college student development, freshman student development, sport psychology and competitive team development; and knowledge and experience in community college programming and services, community resources, residential living and suicide prevention/intervention.

SUMMARY

Master level graduates who want to work with young adults may want to consider a career in counseling on the University level. As stated above there are many different academic and non academic units in which master level graduates are employed. It is important to choose an area and focus ones' academic training and research focus on this area. It will assist students in gaining employment in one of these many units.

REFERENCES

Academic Senate for California Community Colleges, (1997). Standards of Practice for California Community College Counseling Programs. California.

Bond, John M. and Michael V. Woodall. "College/Career Centers: Counselors Successfully at Work." 143 (Spring 1994): 5-9.

Brillant, J. (2001) ESL teaching in collaboration with college counseling. Paper presented at the Annual Meeting of Teacher of English to Speaker of Other Languages, St. Louis, MO.

Broughton, E. (2001). Counseling and support services for college students athletes. Paper presented at the Annual Conference of the American College Personnel Association, Boston MA.

DeStefano, T.J., Petersen, J, Skwerer, L Bickel, S. (2001). Key stakeholders perceptions of the role and functions of college counseling centers. Paper presented at the Annual Conference of the National Association of Student Personnel Administrators, Seattle, WA.

Dill, W. Charles. (1995). Increasing Satisfaction with Career Guidance Services. 149 (Fall 1995): 30-31.

Sandoz, J. (2002). The freshman odyssey: classical metaphors for counseling college students. Paper presented at the Annual Meeting of the American Counseling Association, New Orleans, LA.

Schwartz, A.J. (2006). Are college students more disturbed today? Stability in the acuity and qualitative character of psychopathology of college counseling center clients: 1992-1993 through 2001-2002. Journal of American College Health, Vol. 54, n. 6.

Job Profiles 2003-2009, http://www.jobprofiles.org/eduunicounselor.htm

Wilkipedia Free Encyclopedia, http://en.wikipedia.org/wiki/Student_development

Careers in School Psychology

4

By Kimberly Daniel, Ph.D. and Jennifer West, Ph.D.

Employment Notice

Seeking a dedicated individual with training in school psychology who is committed to working on behalf of school age children in the general and special education settings. This individual must be a team player and enjoy networking, collaborating, and consulting with teachers, school specialists, school administrators, families, community agencies and mental health providers on a variety of issues related to the academic, social, emotional, and behavioral functioning of culturally diverse children. This individual should have experience in administering, scoring, and interpreting the results of a variety of assessments; developing and monitoring early prevention and intervention programs; designing behavioral plans; engaging in short-term counseling and working on crises teams. The applicant should be committed to working with other school personnel to assist schools in providing safe and healthy school environments which support a positive learning environment for diverse school populations.

Applicant should hold at least a 60 semester credit hour master's or specialist's degree in school psychology with relevant field experiences and be certified in school psychology at the national or state level or be eligible for school psychology licensure/certification by the state department of education.

OVERVIEW

The history of the study of children and education can be traced back to the late 1890's (Fagan, 1999) where Lightner Witmer, often considered the father of school psychology, dedicated much of his teaching, training, and research at the University of Pennsylvania towards investigating the psychological principles necessary for understanding and teaching children within schools. The field of school psychology has grown in many directions since that time (Merrell, Ervin, & Gimpel, 2006; Ysseldyke et. al., 2006); however, the common component between school psychology today and that of Witmer's time is a passion for understanding the educational and psychological principles which promote successful learning of our children. If the reader enjoys working with children and is interested in exploring and understanding how to help diverse groups of children thrive educationally, socially, behaviorally and emotionally in schools, then you will be interested in learning about school psychology. The purpose of this chapter is to provide a brief overview of the field of school psychology and to explore the careers available to persons trained at the master's or specialist's level. The information provided in this chapter will briefly: (a) describe the roles and functions of the school psychologist, (b) outline educational requirements and training standards, (c) delineate employment options, and (d) offer advice on issues to consider when applying to graduate programs.

WHO ARE SCHOOL PSYCHOLOGISTS?

School psychologists are professionally trained to collaborate with school personnel, families and community agencies to address the many factors (i.e., academic, social, behavioral, emotional, cultural) that impact student learning (Merrell, Ervin, & Gimpel, 2006; Reschly, 2008). School psychologists typically work in educational settings and work with pre-kindergarten-12th grade students and assist school personnel in evaluating issues and providing approaches to effectively help educate school age children. School psychologists are trained in both education and psychology. They use a variety of approaches and techniques such as assessment and evaluation, consultation, counseling, naturalistic and systematic observations, data analysis, and intervention design to accomplish this goal. While school psychologists often work with individuals, there is a great deal of emphasis towards addressing school-wide and school-system related issues which impact children's learning (Crockett, 2004; Ysseldyke et. al., 2006). While in the past, the work of the school psychologist was reactive, their work today is proactive. The field has emerged from a refer-test-place model to a systems' focused prevention, early intervention, and evidenced-based model (Dawson et. al., 2006; Ysseldyke et. al., 2006). School psychologists are often called upon to respond to questions such as the ones delineated below:

- Would this student benefit from being instructed in a gifted and talented environment?
- Does this student have a learning disability?
- How does a diagnosis of Attention Deficit/Hyperactivity Disorder impact a student's ability to learn in school or get along with their peers?
- What might be the best approach(s) to teaching/instructing this child in class?
- How do we evaluate the seriousness of a suicide threat?
- Which reading program is best for our third grade students?
- What support can you provide this teacher who is having significant difficulties managing her second grade class?
- What are the most effective intervention programs to date in the area of bullying?
- How do we design a more effective approach to educating our increasingly diverse population? How do, we as a system, become more culturally competent and proficient?
- Would you assist in developing a workshop for parents and teachers on self-injurious behaviors in adolescents?

WHAT TYPE OF TRAINING DO I NEED TO BECOME A SCHOOL PSYCHOLOGIST?

Specialized training in the area of school psychology starts at the graduate level. Admittance requirements to school psychology graduate programs vary; thus, it is important to contact the program(s) of interest to find out specifics. Many programs require some undergraduate coursework in psychology. Such coursework might include Learning Theory, Test and Measurements, Child Development, Cognitive Psychology, Statistics and Research Methods, Behavioral Analysis and Abnormal Psychology. Programs may also require some coursework and/ or experience in education (Merrell, Ervin, & Gimpel, 2006). Applicants to school psychology programs often have undergraduate degrees in psychology, but also have degrees and experiences in teaching, special education, child development, and social work (Merrell, Ervin, & Gimpel, 2006).

Credentialing

School psychologists are required to obtain certain credentials prior to engaging in professional practice. Credentialing ensures that the training of professionals meet certain standards prior to going on to practice professionally. These standards are put in place to ensure consistency and to help protect the public. School psychologists secure degrees at the master's, specialist's, and/or doctoral levels. This chapter is geared toward master's and/or specialist's level training. Typically, a minimum of two or three years of training is required to practice in this field. Since many school psychologists work in school systems their training requirements are delineated by the state department of education. States require a master's or a specialist's (typically considered at least 60 hours of graduate training) level credentialed school psychologist to practice in the schools. Many state departments of education model their guidelines for master's and/or specialist's level school psychologists after the training guidelines developed by the National Association of School Psychologists (NASP) entitled the *Standards for Training and*

Field Placement Programs in School Psychology (NASP, 2000b). This model is often adopted in many training programs as they seek approval for or want to maintain national recognition status with NASP. NASP standards advocate at least **three** years of full time study or equivalent to include **60 semester** (or 90 quarter) **hours** of coursework along with a substantial amount of on-site practical field experiences (NASP, 2000b).

Coursework

School psychology majors take coursework in a variety of areas related to school consultation, assessment and evaluation, prevention and intervention, as well as research and planning. Their training often includes coursework in the following areas:

- Psychology and Mental Health
- Psychopathology
- Cognition and Learning
- Human Development
- Education and Instruction
- Special Education Disabilities
- Safety and Crisis Management
- Research Methods and Statistics
- Assessment
- Problem-Solving and Data Management
- Academic and Behavioral Consultation
- Prevention and Intervention Techniques
- School Law and Ethics
- Diversity Awareness

Currently, the National Association of School Psychologists requires NASP approved training preparation programs to provide coursework and/or field experiences in 11 areas identified as domains: Data Based Decision Making and Accountability; Consultation and

Collaboration; Effective Instruction and Development of Cognitive and Academic Skills; Socialization and Development of Life Skills; Student Diversity in Development and Learning; School and System's Organization; Policy Development and Climate; Prevention, Crisis Intervention and Mental Health; Home/School/Community Collaboration; Research and Program Evaluation; School Psychology Practice and Development, and Information Technology (NASP, 2000b).

Fieldwork

Field experiences are embedded throughout the training process (typically identified as Practicum) and then culminate in a **1200 clock hour** supervised Internship experience upon completion of all coursework. At least **54** semester hours (or 81 quarter hours) of coursework must be completed prior to entering the internship. The 1200 clock hour internship should be completed on a full time schedule in a one year period or on a half-time schedule over two consecutive years. A minimum of 600 hours of the internship must be completed in a school setting (NASP, 2000b). Both practicum and internship field experiences are supervised. While practicum requirements may vary from program to program, NASP requirements indicate that school psychology interns must receive at least two hours of weekly supervision from an appropriately credentialed school psychologist in school settings or psychologist in non-school settings.

Each state has different credentialing criteria (i.e., certification or licensure requirements) for school psychologists, it is important to contact the appropriate state board of education to learn about its requirements. Depending on the training program, master's level school psychologists may obtain one or more of the following degrees (NASP, 2007a):

Initials	Title of the Degree
MA	Master of Arts
MS	Master of Science
M.Ed.	Master of Education
CAS	Certificate of Advanced Study
CAGS	Certificate of Advanced Graduate Study
Ed.S	Education Specialist
PsyS	Specialist Degree in School Psychology
SSP	Specialist in School Psychology
NCSP	Nationally Certified School Psychologist

The National Association of School Psychologists also awards a national certification credential that is governed by NASP. Often referred to as a NCSP (i.e., Nationally Certified School Psychologist) certificate, this credential allows recipients to be employed in public school systems as school psychologists in 31 states to date (see NASP website for details: http://www.nasponline.org/certification/statencsp.aspx). School psychologists who obtain national certification status do so because they either have completed a NASP approved graduate training program and obtained a passing score on the Praxis II national examination or they have completed a program similar in structure to that required by NASP, received a passing score on the Praxis II exam, and completed a comprehensive portfolio document as well as a specialized case study.

The Praxis examination is a requirement for the NCSP; yet, it may be optional for state certification in school psychology. The Praxis II is part of the Praxis Series of assessments prepared by and administered through the Educational Testing Service (ETS) for teacher licensure and state certification. The Praxis II assesses knowledge of specific content areas; hence, the Praxis II in school psychology measures knowledge and skills in school psychology. Currently, NASP requires a passing score of 165 (see NASP website for details at: http://www.nasponline.org/certification/etsinfo.aspx). Individuals should also check the state department of education to determine if they require the Praxis II exam.

WHAT CHARACTERISTICS DO EFFECTIVE SCHOOL PSYCHOLOGISTS POSSESS?

Individuals interested in school psychology should consider these factors (Merrell, Ervin, & Gimpel, 2006):

- Do I enjoy working with children and their families?
- Am I interested in understanding human behavior and instruction as it relates to educating children in schools?
- Do I enjoy working in groups and collaborating with others?
- Can I be assertive and yet respectful?
- Am I comfortable working with children who have special needs/disabilities?
- Am I willing to listen to the points of view of others?
- Am I open to learning about and working with individuals who are different than me with respect to race, culture, gender, social economic status, sexual orientation, or religion?
- Do I enjoy engaging in problem-solving activity?
- Do I like collecting, manipulating and analyzing data?
- Do I think critically and use good judgment when making decisions?
- Am I detailed oriented?
- Am I willing to learn about and engage in school related research?
- How well do I organize myself and plan in advance?
- Am I flexible and able to change routine easily?
- Am I an effective listener?
- How effectively do I communicate orally and in writing?
- Do I utilize strategies to manage stressful events/situations?
- Am I willing to engage in ongoing reflection of my professional knowledge, skills and behaviors?

WHAT EMPLOYMENT OPPORTUNITIES ARE AVAILABLE TO PERSONS HOLDING A MASTER'S OR SPECIALIST'S DEGREE IN SCHOOL PSYCHOLOGY?

School Psychologists as Practitioners

The majority of persons with school psychology training work as practitioners in schools (Merrell, Ervin, & Gimpel, 2006; NASP 2007a). They provide a great deal of direct support to children, families and schools. As described above, they perform a variety of duties which include assessment, consultation, and counseling; prevention and intervention support; behavior and crisis management; school-based research; and mental health supports. School Psychology practitioners typically work on special education teams, student support teams, and school climate committees. School psychologists also must be adept at collecting, analyzing, interpreting and summarizing findings both orally and in writing. The goal is to help school age children to succeed academically by addressing issues related to learning, instruction, and social/emotional/behavioral functioning.

School Psychologists as Psychometrists

Persons who have the appropriate training and credentials in this field may work as psychometrists. Psychometrists often work in settings with clinical and neuro-psychologists (see website for National Association of Psychometrist at: http://www.napnet.org/54564. html). However, they can work in schools as well. In schools, persons with the appropriate credentials can administer and score numerous types of psychological, academic, and behavioral assessments under the direct supervision of a licensed or certified school psychologist. The school psychologist can use the data collected by the school psychometrist as a portion of a more comprehensive evaluation. Persons interested in this work should contact their local school systems to inquire about employment opportunities and state level credentialing requirements.

School Psychologists as Administrators and Policy Makers

Some school psychologists advance from their initial role as a school practitioner to an administrative role in the schools (NASP 2007a). They may seek careers in leadership positions such as lead school psychologist, supervisor of school psychological services (although these positions often require a doctorate), assistant principal, or principal, etc. Additional coursework (as well as field experience) in school administration, supervision services, and school law is typically required. Persons may also use their training in school psychology to support careers that enable them to engage in educational and child focused policy development in various governmental agencies as well as local organizations.

School Psychologists as University Lecturers, Adjunct Professors, or Disability Coordinators

School psychologists with appropriate training and experience may be able to secure a position as a part time college or university instructor (NASP, 2000b). Their training and experiences also may open an opportunity for them to work in positions such as the director or coordinator of disability support services, tutorial and/or remedial programs at colleges and universities.

School Psychologists as Associate to Licensed Psychologists in Private Practice

School psychologists trained at the master's or specialist's level typically are unable to engage in private practice. However, they may be able to work as psychological associates under the supervision of a doctoral level psychologist licensed by the State Board of Examiners (as opposed to the State Department of Education) which governs the practice of psychology in states. They can be a valuable asset to the practice as they provide services in consultation, assessment, counseling, research, training, etc., depending on their area(s) of skill and expertise.

School Psychologists as Assistant Researchers

School psychologists with master's degrees could potentially work in research settings at universities, government institutions, policy institutes, clinics, school systems or local agencies (NASP, 2007b). They could assist with activities such as: data collection, management, entry, and analysis. With guidance, they can engage in activities such as: (a) gathering background data for grants; (b) developing surveys and questionnaires; (c) conducting interviews; (d) leading focus groups; or (e) preparing information for presentations. Of course, they could also administer assessments under proper supervision. Coursework and skill development in research methods and statistics, data analysis, assessment, consultation, and interventions could provide background training for one interested in this type of work. One should have a strong interest in research, be detailed oriented, be technologically savvy, be very organized and have excellent skills in writing and speaking.

School Psychologists in Other Roles

Master's level school psychologists possess skills that afford them the opportunity to work in several settings. Obviously, not all positions that utilize the skills of school psychologists have the terms "school" or "psychology" in their position name or description. Individuals with training in this area may use their training to compliment their profession as a special educator, pre-school teacher, consultant, child social worker, educational specialist, behavior specialist, school advocate, juvenile justice worker, etc.

ONCE I OBTAIN MY DEGREE AND SECURE MY JOB, AM I DONE WITH MY TRAINING?

Absolutely not! As with many professions, the field of school psychology is constantly changing. Ongoing research in the field on strategies, techniques and tools; change in national and world events; laws governing policy in education and mental health all have an impact on children. School psychologists have an ethical responsibility to maintain competency in their professional area of training and practice (Jacob and Hartshorne, 2007). According to NASP's Professional Conduct Manual's *Principles of Professional Ethics* (NASP, 2000a):

School psychologists recognize the strengths and limitations of their training and experience, engaging only in practices for which they are qualified. They enlist the assistance of other specialists in a supervisory, consultative, or referral roles as appropriate in providing services. They must continually obtain additional training and education to provide the best possible services to children, families, schools, communities, trainees, and supervisees. (p. 16).

To understand professional development requirements, check with your place of employment and review recertification and licensure requirements at the state level. NASP requires nationally certified school psychologists to obtain 75 hours of professional development training every three years. At least three hours must be in the areas of ethics or professional practice and one third of the hours must be provided by an approved NASP or American Psychological Association (APA) professional development site (see NCSP renewal document at: http://www.nasponline.org/certification/RenewalForms.pdf).

WHAT SHOULD I CONSIDER WHEN APPLYING TO A SCHOOL PSYCHOLOGY PROGRAM?

Below are some suggestions you might consider when exploring school psychology programs:

- Review information about the profession of school psychology
- Reflect on your personal experiences, goals and interests and identify personal expectations for yourself six months, one year, and five years from now
- Consider if a school psychology program will help you meet your goals

- Review the section above listing some of the characteristics school psychologists possess
- Identify university programs of interest and seek out information regarding program structure (i.e., course hours necessary, field work expectations, research requirements, and other activities necessary to graduate); program philosophy and expectations; entry requirements; sequence of courses; typical course loads; class times (i.e., mornings, evenings, weekends, etc.); faculty to student ratio; accreditation; course work; and field and program expectations
- Thoughtfully consider the time you will need to allocate for class, study, group-work, fieldwork, and other obligations such as family and work (if necessary). Include time for rest and renewal
- Consider the size of the program and your access to professors
- Check on sources of financial support (e.g., scholarships, grants, fellowships, loans) and consider how you will manage tuition and other expenses

WHERE CAN I LEARN MORE ABOUT SCHOOL PSYCHOLOGY?

Listed are some activities you can do to find out more about school psychology:

- Review the National Association of School Psychologists' website
- Check to see if you have a state or local school psychologists' association. (The NASP website has a link to state association sites)
- Contact the state department of education and inquire about certification requirements
- Contact your local school system and ask about school psychological services
- Talk to a school psychologist
- Attend a job fair for local school systems

- Peruse university websites regarding school psychology program information
- Contact university training directors and inquire about their programs

The focus of this chapter was to provide the reader some insight into the field and practice of school psychology and to discuss employment opportunities for master's level school psychology professionals. Simply stated, school psychologists strive to engage in activities that promote safe and healthy school environments and academic success. There is a shortage of school psychologists and it is anticipated that the shortage will continue to grow in the next five to 10 years as many school psychologists reach retiring age (Curtis, Grier, & Hunley, 2004; Merrell, Ervin, & Gimpel, 2006; Ysseldyke et. al., 2006). A career in school psychology can be quite fascinating and rewarding but also very challenging. While many school psychologists hold doctoral degrees, the majority of individuals trained in the field hold specialist's degrees (Reschly, 2000; Merrell, Ervin, & Gimpel, 2006). Persons interested in pursuing graduate studies in this area should become familiar with the roles and functions of school psychologists as well as training and credentialing requirements. In addition, they should critically evaluate training programs and explore employment opportunities. Be assertive, do your homework, ask questions, and plan ahead. When pursuing any graduate career path it is very important to take an active role in order to make informed decisions.

REFERENCES

Crockett, D. (2004). Critical issues children face in the 2000s. *School Psychology Review, 33*, 78–82.

Curtis, M.J., Grier, J.E., & Hunley, S. (2004). The changing face of school psychology: Trends in data and projections for the future. *School Psychology Review, 33, 49–66.*

Dawson, M., Cummings, J., Harrison, P., Short, R., Gorin, S., Polamares, R. (2004). The 2002 multisite conference on the future of school psychology: Next steps. *School Psychology Review, 33, 115–125.*

Fagan, T. K. (1999). Training school psychologists before there were school psychologist training programs: A history 1890–1930. In C.R. Reynolds & T.B. Gutkin (Eds.), *The handbook of school psychology* (pp. 2–33). New York: John Wiley and Sons, Inc.

Fagan, T.K. (2008). Trends in the history of school psychology in the United States. In A. Thomas & J. Grimes (Eds.), *Best practices in school psychology V* (pp. 2069–2085). Bethesda, MD: National Association of School Psychologists.

Jacob, S. & Hartshorne, T. (2007). *Ethics and law for school psychologists.* New Jersey: John Wiley and Sons, Inc.

Merrell, K.W., Ervin, R.A., Gimpel, G.A. (2006). *School Psychology for the 21st century: Foundations and practices.* New York: Guilford Press.

National Association of School Psychologists (2000a). Principles of professional ethics: Guidelines for the provision of school psychological services. *Professional Conduct Manual.* Bethesda, MD: Author. Retrieved May 18, 2009 from: http://www.nasponline.org/standards/ProfessionalCond.pdf.

National Association of School Psychologists. (2000b). *Standards for training and field placement programs in school psychology.* Bethesda, MD: Author.

National Association of School Psychologists. (2007a). *A career in school psychology: Selecting a master's, specialist's or doctoral program that meets your needs.* Retrieved May 18, 2009 from: http://www.nasponline.org/students/degreefactsheet.pdf.

National Association of School Psychologists. (2007b). *Alternative career paths for school psychologists.* Retrieved May 18, 2009 from: http://www.nasponline.org/students/Alternative%20Career%20Paths%20FINAL.pdf.

National Association of Psychometrists (n.d.). What is a psychometrist? Retrieved: May 18, 2009 from: http://www.napnet.org/54564.html.

Reschly, D.J. (2000). The present and future status of school psychology in the United States. *School Psychology Review, 29, 507–522.*

Ysseldyke, J., Burns, M., Dawson, P., Kelley, B., Morrison, S., Rosenfield, S., Telzrow, C. (2006). *School psychology: A blueprint for training and practice III.* Bethesda, MD: National Association of School Psychologists.

Drug and Alcohol Counseling as a Career Option

5

By Frank Norton, Ph.D.

T he U.S. Department of Labor's Occupational Outlook Handbook, 2008–09 Edition, indicates that substance abuse counselors' 34% anticipated growth, in the next ten years, is the highest of all growth areas for all counselor career fields. Further, the Maryland Higher Education Commission (MHEC) report dated January 2009 on anticipated workforce shortages, projects a 48% shortfall in Mental Health Counselors and Substance Abuse Counselors for the State of Maryland to continue for some years to come. Clearly, there is a need for substance abuse counselors now and in the future.

Substance abuse/drug addiction is without question a wide and deep problem in American society. In the United States, it plays no favorites and attacks the young and old alike, regardless of any racial or ethnic group or other criteria such as gender, religion, or socioeconomic class (Stevens-Smith & Smith, 1998, p. iii). Alcohol, the leading drug of abuse in this country, alone accounts for 21 % of all hospital admissions to intensive care units (Lieber, 1998). Drug abuse "is a drain not only on the general medical resources of the United States, but also on specialized components of the health care industry" (Doweiko, 2006, pg. 1). Some 85% of all drug problems are associated with the abuse of alcohol—this country's biggest drug problem. Substance abuse is an immense problem that is one of America's most pressing issues and requires an army of drug addiction mental/medical health professionals to attack. Clearly, help is needed in the areas of education, prevention, and treatment from qualified trained professionals.

QUALIFICATIONS TO BECOME A
SUBSTANCE ABUSE COUNSELOR

In the 21st century, credentials for substance abuse counselors are moving upward with more requirements for licensure at the master's level and/or certification at the state and national level. For example, a study of 547 substance abuse counselors in one state found that 42.2% of them had completed a graduate degree and another 8% had some doctoral work and/or completed a doctorate (Culbreth & Borders, 1999). In another study by Kerwin, M. E., Walker-Smith, K.,Kirby, K. (2006), it was found that there are increasingly more states requiring substance abuse counselors to have credentials to function in the addictions field. Their study found 49% of state governments require counseling credentials for substance abuse counselors. Many states, for example, are moving toward a three tier educational requirement that includes either: (1) an associate's degree, (2) bachelor's degree, or (3) a master's degree. All three have educational requirements to be completed in the area of mental health with specialized additional coursework in the area of addictions. These requirements usually include practicum/internship hours working in addictions. To become licensed as a substance abuse counselor, most states require a university degree, such as a master's in counseling, which includes course work and experience in alcohol and other drugs. The State of Maryland, for example, requires a total of 60 credits of master's level courses (whether the master's degree is awarded after the completion of 36, 48, or 60 credits), and 3,000 hours of supervised clinical experience. Maryland also requires exams for drug counselors to become licensed drug counselors (Dolan,1998).

At a broader level, a uniform certification process (Fisher & Harrison, 2005) is being developed by such organizations as the National Association of Alcoholism and Drug Abuse Counselors (NAADAC Certification). They have developed a three tier system: (1) National Certified Addictions Counselor, Level I (NCAC I); (2) National Certified Addiction Counselor, Level II (NCAC II) and (3) Master Addiction Counselor (MAC). At its website (www.naadac.org, 2009) NAADAC estimates that in the next ten years a 35% growth is anticipated in the addictions/behavioral disorder area for counselors. Positions exist for counselors who are trained in drug and alcohol issues from a high school graduate to the doctoral level. The modal degree is now the master's degree in a mental health field, such as counseling or psychology to work in the substance abuse field.

EDUCATIONAL ROUTES TOWARDS SUBSTANCE ABUSE LICENSURE

What follows is a route towards becoming licensed at the master's level as an addictions counselor. Most of these programs have a requirement of a total of 36 to 60 credit hours to earn the master's degree. Many candidates enter the master's program with a bachelor's degree in a related social science field such as psychology, nursing, or social work and related experience working in the mental health field. Once in the master's program, they complete courses preparing them to become a counselor. Course work is geared towards preparing the candidate to gain knowledge in a wide arena to include group therapy, family dynamics, multicultural issues, career counseling and groundwork in theories of counseling, psychopathology and ethics. Included are practical experiences via practicum and internship placements in the local communities where the candidate performs duties at work sites under the supervision of a licensed mental health practitioner. Work sites might include an inpatient facility, residential half way house, or private or government outpatient agency. For those not seeking licensure, there are national certification credentials that some work agencies accept in lieu of a license. Those national level credentials can be found in a later section of this chapter under "National Certification and/or Licensure."

SPECIALIZED TRAINING IN SUBSTANCE ABUSE

Drug & Alcohol Counseling: Working with substance abusers requires specialized training about drugs, whether it be learning about prescribed medications, alcohol or an illegal drug—all can affect the biological, psychological, social and spiritual world of an individual. Sorting out which component is being affected by drugs is difficult. Each chemical of abuse can cause different effects on the individual often making it difficult to ascertain if what you are observing is psychological and/or biologically induced behavior. Often, it is a combination. For example, an individual in withdrawal from alcohol may look like he/she is anxious and/or depressed. Is what you are observing depression or is it the withdrawal effects from drugs causing symptoms that look like depression? Or is it an interaction between drugs and mood? Further complicating the picture is that the intellect may be affected adversely by chemical abuse. It is not uncommon to see a patient that looks intellectually impaired from drugs who may improve significantly after a few months of sobriety. Thus, these complications make it difficult to obtain accurate information on current patient status. What is due to drug withdrawal? What is due to complications from physical damage already done from past drug abuse? What other drugs may be interacting with alcohol to induce the behavior you are observing? For that matter, does the patient even know or remember what he/she has taken? Counseling skill development in the area of substance abuse thus requires knowledge of multiple areas of possible factors effecting current behavior. Course knowledge is needed in such courses as Drug & Alcohol Counseling, Abnormal Psychology, Counseling Techniques, Theories on Counseling and Psychopharmacology.

PSYCHOPHARMACOLOGY

Closely related to drugs of abuse is the need to know how medications prescribed to help substance abusers interact with their history of addiction. Just the seemingly deceptive easy task of gathering intake information is froth with uncertainty in data gathering. It is not uncommon to have the client not remember what or how much, how often and how long they were taking a drug as memory deficits are a common side effect of abusing drugs. Medication planning is most often then, sometimes a hit or miss affair. Given their history of drug abuse, careful planning is needed to insure newly prescribed drugs do not trigger a relapse. The fact that most physicians are not trained to cope with recovery substance abusers further complicates the issue of obtaining information to plan a successful recovery. In one study, 94% of physicians who reviewed case histories did not correctly identify alcohol abuse as the probable cause of the patient's problem. In the same study done by the National Center on Addiction and Substance Abuse at Columbia University (2000), only 20% of the physicians canvassed felt they could deal with alcoholics. Less than 17% felt they had the skills needed to cope with prescription drug abusers. Also, the issue that medication abuse needs continuous monitoring must be taken into account with recovering drug abusers. For example, they may become re-addicted to prescription medications given to them after surgery for pain control. There are also gender specific issues to consider in psychopharmacology treatment. For example, women's main drugs of choice are the drugs of alcohol and medication, primarily sedatives and stimulants (Ortiz, A., Soriano, A, Meza, D., Martinez, R., Galvan, J. 2008). Both sedative and stimulant medications have abuse potential and re-addictions issues that a physician must sort out. Thus, it can be seen that part of the job of a substance abuse counselor is attempting to connect their patients with physicians/psychiatrists who are knowledgeable about drugs of abuse and medications to treat those in recovery. Such connections with qualified physicians/psychiatrists are not easily done as the list is short of well informed physicians on addictions. Counselors need to take at least one major course in Psychopharmacology to be able to effectively communicate with physicians and at least be aware of what classes of drugs a substance abuser is using, their side effects, and normal dosage levels.

ASSESSMENT, EVALUATION & INTAKE SKILL DEVELOPMENT

Substance abuse counselors need to learn short assessment and screening instruments that are valid and reliable that can elicit a lot of information quickly. The simpler the questions, the more likely the addict can answer them and provide valid results. Counselors need to learn such instruments to help them assess clients/patients and plan an effective treatment plan. A short and valid assessment instrument is the CAGE where each letter stands for a key question asked to the client (Dowieko, 2006). It consists of four questions:

1. Have you ever felt you ought to **Cut** down on your drinking and/or drugging?
2. Have people **Annoyed** or **Angered** you by criticizing your drinking?
3. Have you ever felt bad or **Guilty** about your drinking?
4. Have you ever had a drink first thing in the morning to steady your nerves or to get rid of a hangover (**EYE**-OPENER)?

To answer even one of these questions in the affirmative needs intensive follow-up by the examiner/counselor. The CAGE is an instrument that is highly favored by medical insurance companies who like its apparent simplicity. The CAGE is also a good jumping off point to discuss with the substance abuser their alcohol and other drug use. Another self report instrument that is also used frequently is the MAST (Michigan Alcoholism Screening Test). It consists of 24 questions which can be answered with either a "yes" or "no."

Both instruments are good screening tools that provide quick information on alcohol and other drug dependence issues. They both are rough screening tools without sensitivity to subtle differences between substance abuse and/or dependence, remembering again that alcohol is the number one drug of abuse in this country. They are excellent for a quick look at possible alcohol dependency issues. Some education thus is needed by taking an assessment course on testing and learning how to interpret tests by master's level substance abuse counselors.

More in-depth assessment instruments require knowledge gained through graduate level courses include the Substance Abuse Subtle Screening Inventory (SASSI) which is one page long, highly accurate and has adolescent and adult norms and includes a Spanish version. Also, the Dissociative Experiences Scale (DES; Bernstein & Putnam, 1986) can be given by master's level counselors is an instrument whose validity and reliability have been well demonstrated to tap into dissociative symptoms often found in substance abusing populations. The Drug Abuse Screening Test (DAST) is another useful test often used in conjunction with the CAGE or MAST. It does not focus on alcohol but rather other drugs of abuse and has robust internal consistency, test-retest reliability and concurrent validity (Gavin & Skinner, 1989). A very useful test to give substance abusers is the Beck Depression Inventory which has good reliability and validity in measuring depression. Graduate students planning to work in substance abuse thus need to take at least one course in Tests & Measurements and/or Appraisal, Assessment, & Evaluation and an undergraduate course in Statistics.

TREATING THE DUAL DIAGNOSED: TRAUMA/POST TRAUMATIC STRESS DISORDER TRAINING

One of the most common diagnoses co-occurring with substance abuse is Post Traumatic Stress Disorder (PTSD). Some studies show that the rate of substance abuse in people with PTSD may be as high as 60–80% (Donovan & Padin-Rivera, 1999). Particularly associated with PTSD are high rates of childhood physical and/or sexual abuse (Najavits, Weiss, & Shaw, (1997). Research findings suggest that trauma survivors in many cases abuse substances as a chemical anesthesia that will numb feelings and perhaps protect them for awhile from psychological distress. Later, what these individuals discover is that their symptoms of withdrawal become associated with their PTSD triggers and cause even more distress to them (Doweiko, 2006). Although substance abuse can lead to victimization, in too many cases, evidence exists that the substance use began after the trauma and the development of PTSD (NIDA, 2002). As can be seen by the above, addictions counselors need to develop clinical skills in multiple areas to best help their client population. For an excellent review of common aspects of treatment for PTSD and concurrent addiction issues, this author recommends Najavits' (1999) article review on clinical guidelines for treatment.

Another study (Windle, Windel, Scheidt, & Miller, 1995) found that 49% of women in alcohol inpatient programs and 12% of men had a history of some form of sexual abuse in their past. After collecting data for a twenty year period of an adolescent female residential program, Wallace (1993) reported that fully 90% of their teens had a history of sexual abuse. Wallace and her staff then developed a group based dual diagnosed program to help their adolescent females. Dr. Nora Volkow, Director of the National Institute on Drug Abuse (NIDA), states that PTSD and the co-morbid disorder of substance abuse of "returning military members and other veterans" (Price, 2009, p. 22) are emerging trends that need mental health interventions. Courtois (1999) in her excellent book, *Recollections of Sexual Abuse: Treatment Principles and Guidelines,* offers the therapist practical and "supportive neutrality towards the patient ..." (pg. xvii) and suggestions on dealing with this difficulty issue. Counselors thus need to gain knowledge on PTSD and how sexual abuse issues in the treating of many substance abusers.

There is a large overlap between mental health disorders and substance abuse/dependency. Surprisingly, most treatment programs are not geared to treat both at the same time, but rather play what this author calls "ping-pong" treatment of patients with substance abuse issues and an ongoing mental health disorder. For example, this author has had experiences where an individual who is in an addictions unit for treatment and is discovered to have a serious mental health problem is usually transferred out of the unit. The attempt is then made to place them on a psychiatric unit which usually refuses the patient because they have a substance abuse problem. Sometimes the patient ends up with no help and falls through the crack of a system geared to treat only one problem at a time. This practice is slowly changing in some cases. Courtois (2006) who runs an inpatient dissociative disorders unit in Washington, D.C., accepts addicts if they are dual diagnosed and treats both at the same time. Hers is a much more clinical appropriate approach that is consistent with the National Institute of Drug Abuse (NIDA, 2009) guidelines on treatment of substance abuse individuals. Graduate students need course work then in such areas as Human Growth & Development, Diagnosis & Psychopathology, and Individual Counseling Techniques.

ASAM (AMERICAN SOCIETY OF ADDICTIONS MEDICINE) CRITERIA

Most medical insurance forms require that the American Society of Addictive Medicine (ASAM) criteria be used to determine placement of a patient for chemical abuse treatment. It is also used by hospitals to make decisions on whether a substance abuser needs outpatient or inpatient care. ASAM criteria uses five possible levels (ASAM, 2001), with one being geared towards adolescents and the other for adults. Criteria moves from least resource needs (outpatient care) to most intensive and greater need for resources such as medical complications from drug abuse combined with perhaps dual diagnosed issues (inpatient care). Criteria are measured along six dimensions according to ASAM's Revised Patient Placement Criteria (ASAM PPC-2R) released in April of 2001. The six admission criteria are:

- Acute intoxication/withdrawal potential.
- Biomedical conditions and complications.
- Emotional, behavioral or cognitive conditions and complications.
- Readiness to change;
- Relapse, continued use or continued problem potential.
- Recovery environment the patient must face.

Diagnostic terminology for ASAM PPC-2R is compatible with DSM-IV-TR (Diagnostic and Statistical Manual of Mental Disorders—Text Revised, 2002). All mental health professionals, regardless of whether or not they are addictions counselors, need to be familiar with ASAM PPC-2R criteria and levels of care. Perhaps surprisingly to some, most mental health professionals are not familiar with ASAM criteria.

DSM-IV-TR SUBSTANCE DIAGNOSES AND DUAL DIAGNOSES

Familiarity with DSM-IV-TR is needed for payment in private practice and funding agencies billing medical insurance. All five axis of DSM-IV-TR must be completed in detail on each patient/client and revised as the patient progresses through treatment. For private practice counselors working with dual diagnosed clients, knowledge of co-morbid disorders involving substance issues is essential for successful treatment. Particularly needed is the development of strong assessment skills to probe for multiple DSM-IV-TR co-occurring diagnoses often found with substance abusers. On admission, it is not uncommon for substance abusers to focus on their current issues and avoid discussing past trauma. Skill is needed to obtain the broadest and most comprehensive picture of their patient/client. Such in-depth analysis leads to better treatment. Seen frequently, as mentioned earlier, are patients/clients who have a substance abuse diagnosis and a mental health diagnosis such as PTSD, depression and/or an anxiety disorder. Master's level counselors need to be familiar with both diagnostic groups and treatment approaches needed to help their patient/client. Research (NIDA, 1999) has found that the most effective treatment is to see the patient as having multiple needs that demand to be addressed at various phases of treatment. They may include dual diagnoses, legal, financial, family, vocational and/or coping skills development.

FAMILY THERAPY

For every person abusing alcohol, it is estimated that four other people are adversely affected by their abuse, especially family and friends (Vick, Smith, & Herrera, 1998). Often, family members no longer see what is happening around them as a family member sinks into substance abuse. Adaptation by their family usually occurs to the pathological behavior of the abuser and family members adjust to roles necessitating it. Family therapy is thus often indicated in many of these cases to uncover what each family member's role is in their adaptation to their substance abusing member. Therapy also helps family members recognize patterns of behavior that are not helpful to their family and learn more adaptive means to help each other. Individual family members often experience trauma from their substance abusing members and need help to become less traumatized and more aware of their choices to lead more productive lives for themselves. Sometimes, the family of origin is so toxic that consideration should be given to help the client/patient disengage and create their own family network. Obvious perhaps is the need to receive training in Family Counseling, Group Counseling and Human Growth & Development.

COUNSELORS IN RECOVERY

Does being in recovery make you a better counselor? Research findings strongly suggest that well trained counselors, regardless of whether or not they are recovering substance abusers themselves, are just as effective in counseling substance abusers. This is consistent with prior research on what makes an effective counselor (Gladding, 2004). In other words, counselor skills learned cross over into becoming a substance abuse counselor. Effective counselors are individuals who have competencies in balancing interpersonal, technical and scientific knowledge into their skill repertoire (Cormier & Cormier, 1998). Such skills enhance a counselor developing competency in addictions counseling once the counselor has gained experience and supervision on working with addicts. A study by Culbreth and Borders (1999) surveyed 547 substance abuse counselors who were either in recovery themselves or nonrecovering counselors. They found that the recovery status of the counselor made no difference in their satisfaction with supervision from a recovered or non recovered supervisor. From the patients point of view, another study found that mid forties female counselors in addictions units were just as effective, from the patient's point of view, as recovered addiction counselors in helping them. The same study found objective procedures and protocols used to measure patient progress were no different for either group, and that, recovered addicts who were substance abuse counselors were just as effective as substance abuse counselors who had no personal addictions issues of their own in treating patients. In Fisher & Harrison's substance abuse textbook (2005) Miller (1995) is quoted as stating "The effectiveness of counselors has been found to be unrelated to whether or not they are themselves 'in recovery' (p. 94)."

SPECIALIZED POPULATIONS SERVED

In working with substance abuse populations, clinical skill development is needed in various populations such as children or adolescents to understand some of the unique aspects of that particular population. For example, children and adolescents who have substance abuse issues have often been exposed to family members who have used and abused drugs. Therapy, as mentioned earlier, often requires family involvement to change the system the children/or adolescents must deal with until they are old enough to be on their own. Choices must also be made by these youths on how much and who they wish to associate with as peers, friends and family members as they learn skills needed to maintain their sobriety and/or drug free life style. School problems are also often present and need to be addressed. Adults also offer particular unique challenges for counselors who choose to work with that population as well as women, people of color, geriatrics, gays and lesbians and other minorities. For example, geriatric patients are often also dealing with grief at the loss of loved ones, loneliness, shrinking social support systems, less income, and more health and aging issues. Counseling theories courses are needed that cover major theoretical schools of treatment for diverse populations and how to apply them is also needed.

CAREER PATHS

The U.S. Department of Labor, Bureau of Labor Statistics, 2008–09 Edition, states counselors in 2006 were working in some 635,000 jobs of which 83,000 were in the substance abuse field (See Attachment 1). They report that a strong demand will continue for substance abuse counselors particularly with the growth of drug courts instead of jail sentences for drug abusers. Also, they note that insurance companies are more inclined to reimburse master's level counselors in private practices or agencies because it is a cost savings compared to paying psychologists/psychiatrists. They project a need for some 29,000 additional substance abuse counselors by 2016, a 34% increase over present numbers. Government agencies at various levels such as the county, state, and federal offer opportunities for individuals to learn skills needed to become an effective substance abuse counselor. Practicum and internship experiences are also valuable ways of gaining understand and skills needed to work with substance abuse issues. Non-profit agencies and for profit agencies as well as private self support substance abuse programs offer a varied population for those counselors interested in the field of addictions. Employee Assistance Programs (EAP), pastoral programs, private practice and teaching also are areas that offer the addictions counselor an environment where they can make a difference in helping others.

STRESS, BURNOUT & SELF CARE ISSUES

Turnover of counselors is an issue in the substance abuse field. It is driven by many diverse factors. These include programs that are inadequately funded, overextension of counselors to meet overwhelming needs with inadequate resources and the resulting burnout of addictions counselors. The need is great and many counselors find they cannot alone cope with it (Ducharme, L.J., Knudsen, H.K. & Roman, P.M., 2008).

Part of the problem is the training of counselors themselves often leads them to attempt to do too much on their own. What the counselors need is support for themselves and the assistance of the community to help substance abusers. What has become obvious to the reader of this chapter is that treatment needs exceed limited resources available. As is evident from this review, drug abuse is a national problem with limited resources allocated to deal with it. Of the money spent by the federal government, an excessive proportion has gone to interdiction, i.e. the "war on drugs" and not enough on education and prevention according to the National Institute on Drug Abuse (NIDA, 2001). For every dollar spent on education/prevention, the National Institute on Drug Abuse (NIDA) estimates a return of 8 dollars as opposed to interdiction results lowering substance abuse in this country. Given the limited resources available and based on effective treatment approaches, what is needed is an emphasis on education and prevention as primary means of lowering chemical abuse.

For counselors, stress and burnout can be lowered by realizing they alone cannot help the chemical abusers. What is needed is a team approach, often called the interdisciplinary or multidisciplinary approach. Here, the addictions counselor often becomes the case manager helping connect the patient with needed resources. Such resources include, but are not limited to self-help groups (AA/NA, Ala-non), vocational counseling, legal assistance, nutritionists, and medical team members involved with health care issues. By the counselor obtaining support from other team members, burn out is reduced and the patient receives more help in staying clean and sober. For example, in a survey of 1,800 substance abuse counselors, Ducharme et al (2008) emotional exhaustion and intent to quit their jobs was inversely related to their support system with coworkers.

Counselors also need to make time for themselves, such as exercise, hobbies not related to work, and practice good sleep hygiene and nutrition. Being a role model for the patient often teaches their clients/patients more than words that they also need to improve their own care.

USE OF COMMUNITY RESOURCES

In this author's opinion, for many substance abusers, it literally requires a whole village to assist their recovery to include family counseling, individual counseling, group counseling, self-help groups like AA/NA, an AA sponsor, nutritionists, physicians to deal with health/medication issues etc. Thus, to be effective as a substance abuse counselor for your clients, it is necessary to help them connect to resources in the community as mentioned under burnout and stress reduction. Such resources include but are not limited to legal assistance, financial help, job training, child care, housing and support groups such as AA/NA. A counselor cannot do it alone and if they try they will burnout. In many cases, it can take years for a substance abuser to obtain help. Until then, they are often losing family support, friends, getting into legal difficulties, and having job difficulties.

Part of being an effective counselor is to learn what community resources exist and matching them with your recovering clients needs. Also, included in the process of recovery is having the counselor also teach relapse prevention skills to the substance abuser. In this case, "forwarned is for-armed" helps the client learn skills needed in the recovery process. Research by NIDA (1999) indicates that effective treatment means effective follow up of the multiple needs of recovering substance abusers. This recovery includes a strong relapse prevention plan. Use of self help groups such as AA/NA, a sponsor in AA/NA, is often encouraged by treatment programs as part of the relapse plan very early in their recovery. Advantages for clients are that such self help groups are free and offer them fellowship and support. It is also a resource for counselors in that it offers the addict feedback which later can then be processed in individual and/or group therapy. As there is a trend in this country towards shorter treatment time and away from inpatient to outpatient programs to save money, AA and other self help groups offer longer term assistance to the substance abuser if they wish it. AA is an effective support system for the chemically dependent (Taylor, 2005). For many, faith based organizations are also a source of tremendous support. Courses need would include Addictions Treatment Delivery, Family Counseling and Group Counseling.

Funding trends for substance abuse treatment have changed over time. Government support of addictions treatment in the 1950s was minimal but geared up in the late 1960s as the flower generation and military soldiers returning from Viet Nam experienced increased drug abuse issues. Initially, outpatient treatment was attempted, but quickly shifted to inpatient care. The result was an increased need for counselors and other trained mental health professionals to assist in treating chemically dependent individuals. Government funding was then expanded to train mental health professionals in addictions and expand resources both in the community and in outpatient and inpatient settings. Inpatient hospital care, although still available, has decreased in the last 15 years as medical insurance has cut benefits associated with their care. The result has been a shift to more outpatient and community care programs. Often, care is now affected by a combination of funding sources to include reimbursement provided by private and government funding sources. These include grants, faith based treatment agencies, program funding from States to include Medicare/Medicaid, and third party payments from private insurance plans.

STATE LICENSURE REQUIREMENTS

Substance abuse counselor licensure requirements vary by state. Licensure by a state is considered a higher credential that certification and general requires more course work. Outlined below are the licensure requirements at the master's level for substance abuse counselors in the State of Maryland.

1. a master's degree with 60 graduate semester credits in a counseling field from an accredited college or university.
2. At least 25 credits in alcohol & drug training which may include:
   • Pharmacology
   • Individual counseling techniques
   • Group counseling
   • Abnormal psychology
   • Addictions Treatment Deliver
   • Topics in Alcohol & Drug Dependency

- Family Counseling
- Theories of Counseling/psychotherapy
- Human Growth & Development
- Diagnosis & Psychopathology
- Psychotherapy & the Treatment of Mental and Emotional Disorders
- Drug & alcohol counseling and finally
- A 3 credit course in ethics which must include a section on drug and alcohol counseling.

NATIONAL CERTIFICATION AND/OR LICENSURE

The National Association of Addiction Professionals (NAADAC) has developed a national standard for uniform certification. It is an independent national body certifying educational and training requirements for substance abuse counselors. Its highest credential MAC (Master Addictions Counselor) requires a current master's degree in nursing, social work, psychology, counseling, or other helping professions. It also requires 500 clock hours of training and education with specific training being obtained in drug abuse counseling. Also, the individual must have a current state license or certificate in their profession such as a Licensed Professional Counselor, Licensed Psychologist and/or Social Worker. Additionally, applicants for the MAC must have three years of supervised clinical experience, of which two years are acquired after obtaining their master's degree.

Examination by NAADAC is provided. For the MAC licensure national exam, three areas are tested and they are (1) Pharmacology of Addictive Substances, (2) Counseling Practices and (3) Professional Issues.

Other mental health provides such as physicians, psychologists, social workers and other helping professions can also receive a NAADAC qualification as a Substance Abuse Professional (SAP). Although not a certification or license, The SAP qualification allows those in the health and human services counseling field to evaluate Department of Transportation (DOT) government workers for follow-up care if needed.

Another agency, the National Board for Certified Counselors (NBCC) has developed an Examination for Master Addictions Counselors (EMAC). The NBCC, a non-profit agency, is a nationally recognized organization that offers licensure exams that acceptable by most states. The NBCC is an agency that helps to set the standards for the general practice of counseling professionals to include specialty areas like substance abuse counseling. The EMAC has five subject content areas that are tested. They are (1) Assessment, (2) Counseling Practices, (3) Treatment Process, (4) Treatment Planning and Implementation and (5) Prevention.

The International Certification & Reciprocity Consortium/Alcohol Other Drug Abuse, Inc. (IC&RC) is another certifying body. Exams or testing are not given by them. Rather, it is group of agencies that certify someone has credentialing or licensing in alcohol and other drug abuse areas such as clinical supervisors, prevention specialists, co-occurring professionals and criminal justice professionals. The importance of the IC&RC's endorsement is that 44 states, other federal government agencies such as the Department of Transportation and the Department of Defense, and 12 global jurisdictions recognize its stamp of approval of substance abuse certification/licensure. Thus, IC&RC endorsement allows portability of certification/license to other jurisdictions. For example, a substance abuse counselor from a state accepting the IC&RC credential could accept a job in another state or government agency. Then, their NBCC MAC exam results could be transferred to an agency having an agreement with IC&RC. The advantage is the individual not having to retake the exam in the new state or agency. However, the mental health provider must still pass the state exam regarding laws and regulations, which can vary state to state (Norton & Jeter, 2009).

SUMMARY

In summary, the career field of addictions has grown significantly. It is projected to continue to grow in the future. Drug courts nationwide have grown immensely in the past fifteen years offering hope that treatment is more important than warehousing addicts in jails (Levinthal, 2006). More well-trained counselors are needed with an ever widening range of skills. Substance abuser counselors now need to not only know how to treat substance abuse itself, but need to know how to deal with dual diagnosed clients with issues such as PTSD. Knowledge of medications is especially critical for a substance abuse counselor to communicate with physicians and to know how medication affects their clients. In many cases, family involvement is necessary to increase the chances of a successful recovery process. Relapse prevention skills is needed and most importantly, compassion, patience and acceptance of your clients.

REFERENCE

American Psychiatric Association. (2002). *Diagnostic and statistical manual of mental disorders* (4th ed., Text Revision). Washington, DC: American Psychiatric Association.

American Society of Addiction Medicine. (2001). *The ASAM patient placement criteria for the treatment of substance-related disorders. 2nd Ed. Revised. (ASAM PPC-2R).*

Bernstein, E.M., & Putnam, F.W. (1986). Development, reliability, and validity of a dissociative scale. *Journal of Nervous and Mental Disease, 174,* 727–735.

Culbreth, John R., Borders, L. DiAnne (1999). *Perceptions of the supervisory relationship: Recovering and nonrecovering substance abuse counselors.* Journal of Counseling & Development, Vol. 77, 330–338.

Center for Substance Abuse Research (CESAR), University of Maryland, College Park, Aug. 16, 2004, Vol. 13, Issue 33.

Cormier, L.S., & Cormier, W. H. (1998). *Fundamental skills and cognitive behavioral interventions* (4th ed.). Pacific Grove, CA: Brooks/Cole.

Courtois, Christine (1998), *Healing the incest wound: adult survivors in therapy.* W.W. Norton & Co., New York, NY.

Courtios, Christine (1999). *Recollections of sexual abuse: Treatment principles and guidelines.* W.W. Norton & Co., New York, NY.

Dolan, Dallas M. (1998). *Certification for drug and alcohol counselors.* Department of Health and Mental Hygiene, State of Maryland web site.

Donova, B. & Padin-Rivera, E. (1999). *Transcend: A program for treating PTSD and substance abuse in Vietnam combat veterans.* NC-PTSD Clinical Quarterly, 8, 3, pp. 51–53.

Doweiko, H. (2006). Concepts of Chemical Dependency, Brooks/Cole, 6th Ed.

Ducharme, L.J., Knudsen, H.K. & Roman, P.M. (2008). *Emotional exhaustion and turnover in human service occupations: The protective role of coworkers support.* Sociological Spectrum, 28 (1), 81–104.

Fisher, Gary L. & Harrison, Thomas C. (2005). *Substance abuse, information for school counselors, social workers, therapists, and counselors.* (3rd ed.). Allen & Bacon.

Gavin, D.R., Ross, H.E., Skinner, H.A. (1989). Diagnostic validity of the Drug Abuse Screening Test in the assessment of DSM-III drug disorders, *British J. of Addiction,* 84 (3), 301–307.

Gladding, Samuel. (2004). *Counseling, a comprehensive profession.* New York: Macmillan publishing company. 5th ed.

Kerwin, M. E., Walker-Smith, K.,Kirby, K. (2006). Comparative analysis of state requirements for the training of substance abuse and mental health counselors. *Journal of Substance Abuse Treatment,* 30, 173–181.

Levinthal, C. (2006). *Drugs, society, and criminal justice.* Allyn and Bacon. 1st ed., Boston, MA.

Lieber, C.S. (1998). Hepatic and other medical disorders of alcoholism: From pathogenesis to treatment. *Journal of Studies on Alcohol,* 59 (1), 9–25.

Miller, W.R., & Hester, R.K. (1995). *Treatment for alcohol problems: Towards an informed eclecticism.* In R.K. Hester & W. R. Miller (Eds.), Handbook of alcoholism treatment approaches: Effective alternatives (2md ed., pp. 89–104). Boston: Allyn & Bacon.

Najavits, L.M., Weiss, R.D., and Shaw, S.R. (1997). *The link between substance abuse and posttraumatic stress disorder in women: A research review.* The American Journal on Addictions, 6, 273–283.

Najavits, L. (1999). *Seeking safety: A new cognitive-behavioral therapy for PTSD and substance abuse.* Clinical Quarterly, Summer. Vol. 8, Issue 3.

National Center on Addiction and Substance Abuse at Columbia University. (2000). *CASA releases physician survey.* Press release, May 10.

National Institute on Drug Abuse. (1999). *Thirteen principles of effective drug addiction treatment. NIDA Notes.* Vol. 14, Number 5, December.

National Institutes of Health (2002). *NIDA community drug alert bulletin: Stress & substance abuse.* Washington DC, National Clearinghouse for Alcohol and Drug Information.

Norton, F. & Jeter, R. (2009). Certification and licensing of substance abuse counselors. Encyclopedia of Substance Abuse Prevention, Treatment, and Recovery, Sage Publications, 169–172.

(Ortiz, A., Soriano, A, Meza, D., Martinez, R., Galvan, J. 2008). *Substance abuse among men and women: Similarities and differences.* In Results of Information Reporting System on Drugs, Salud Mental 29 (5): 32–37.

Price, M. (2009). *Emerging trends in addiction treatment.* Monitor on Psychology, American Psychological Association, March, Vol. 40, No.3.

Stevens-Smith, P.,& Smith, R.I. (1998). *Substance abuse counseling: Theory and practice.* Upper Saddle "River, NJ: Merrill/Prentice Hall.

Taylor, Purcell. (2005). *Diagnosis & treatment of substance-related disorders: The DECLARE model.* Allen & Bacon.

U.S. Department of Labor, Occupational Outlook Handbook, 2008–2009 Edition obtained from www.bis.gov/oco/ocos067.htm.

Vick, R.D., Smith, L.M., & Herrera, C.I.R. (1998). The healing circle: An alternative path to alcoholism recovery. *Counseling and Values,* 42, 133–141.

Wallace, S. (1993). Caritas House for adolescent females. Presentation at NECAD (North East Conference on Alcohol & Drugs), Newport, R.I.

Windle, M., Windle, R.C., Scheidt, D.M., Miller, G.B. (1995). Physical and sexual abuse and associated mental disorders among alcoholic inpatients, *American Journal of Psychiatry,* 152, 1322–1328.

Projections data from the National Employment Matrix

Occupational title	SOC Code	Employment, 2006	Projected employment, 2016	Change, 2006-16	
				Number	Percent
Counselors	21-1010	635,000	771,000	136,000	21
Substance abuse and behavioral disorder counselors	21-1011	83,000	112,000	29,000	**34**
Educational, vocational, and school counselors	21-1012	260,000	292,000	33,000	13
Marriage and family therapists	21-1013	25,000	32,000	7,400	30
Mental health counselors	21-1014	100,000	130,000	30,000	30
Rehabilitation counselors	21-1015	141,000	173,000	32,000	23
Counselors, all other	21-1019	27,000	32,000	4,500	17

*Source: U.S. Department of Labor, Bureau of Labor Statistics, Occupational Outlook Handbook, 2008–09 Edition

Mental Health Career Opportunities in Correctional Facilities

6

By Otis Williams, III, Ph.D.

Over the past three decades, the United States has witnessed a dramatic increase in prison population (Bureau of Justice Statistics, 2008; Hamlett, 2006; Institute of Medicine, 2007; Lynch, 2007; Reese, 2006; Wood, 2003). Despite comprising only five percent of the world's population, the U.S. holds a quarter of the world's prisoners. In the 1990's, during an era of presumably industrial and technological advancement, the U.S. experienced its fastest growing incarceration rate in history. Remarkably, the prison rate doubled three times in the previous twenty-seven years. In 2005, there were approximately 1.4 million men and women imprisoned in state and federal institutions. Currently, the U.S. has the largest prison population and highest incarceration rate in the world (Institute of Medicine, 2007; Lynch, 2007). It is estimated that, by year 2010, the U.S. prison population will well surpass 2 million inmates (Lynch, 2007). However, with the inclusion of local jails, the inmate population currently exceeds 2.3 million (Bureau of Justice Statistics, 2008).

Not surprisingly, given the above statistics, the prison industry has been the fastest growing economic enterprise in the United States since the 1990's (Alexander, 2000). On the list of *Fortune 500* companies, only General Motors has employed more people than the prison industry. With the recent proliferation in inmate population and new facilities, prison employment has also expanded faster than any other workforce segment within the government (Alexander, 2000; Boothby & Clements, 2002). As of 2002, the rate of hiring within correctional facilities is at a record high (Boothby & Clements, 2002). Notwithstanding this fact, the demand, recruitment, and need for personnel, such as correctional officers, case managers, and health care professionals, continues to grow and is a major undertaking. Among mental health professionals in particular, career opportunities are more propitious than in the past. As we shall examine, the percentage of inmates with mental illness has soared parallel to that of the expansion of the general prison population. For a myriad of reasons beyond the scope of this current chapter, correctional facilities have become the nation's leading mental health institution (Fagan & Ax, 2003; Scott & Gerbasi, 2005). Theoretically, as the mentally ill population increases; thus, the need for mental health services and professionals will continue to increase.

Boothby and Clements (2002) tracked the number of mental health professionals working in corrections over the past 25 years. The authors noted a steady rise in master's and doctoral level psychologists working in corrections. During the early 1980's, there was an estimated 600 psychologists employed by state and federal facilities. In 1992, approximately ten years later, the number had risen to merely 1,100 psychologists. Currently, it is estimated that over 2,000 psychologists are working in corrections. This total is expected to expand with the recent growth of interest among students in the field of forensic psychology. Boothby and Clements (2002) reported that enrollment in related forensic psychology/criminal justice courses have noticeably increased among undergraduate students throughout the country. Moreover, among graduate students, applications for clinical training and research have soared in the field of forensic psychology. Similarly, this trend is evident among doctoral students as well; whereby, more correctional facilities are offering pre-doctoral clinical internship rotations (Boothby & Clements, 2002).

MENTAL ILLNESS AND THE CORRECTIONS' POPULATION

According to Darrell A. Reiger, M.D., M.P.H., deputy medical director of the American Psychiatric Association, "prisons are the largest mental health institutions in our country" (as cited in Institute of Medicine,

2007, p. 44). Over the past three decades, prisons and jails have become the new mental asylums (Institute of Medicine, 2007; Kupers, 1999). At the same time, while the number of inmates with mental illness has increased, there has been a continual decline in persons institutionalized in state mental health hospitals in the United States (Fagan, 2003; Scott & Gerbasi, 2005). A cursory review of the data suggests an urgent need for the presence and services of mental health professionals in corrections. Data from the Bureau of Justice Statistics (2006) indicate that over 50 percent of all prison and jail inmates have mental health problems, which is based on two criteria: (a) a recent history of; or (b) symptoms of a mental health problem within the past 12 months. Statistics further indicate that approximately 43% of state inmates and 54% of jail inmates, respectively, meet the criteria for mania. An estimated 23% of state inmates and 30% of jail inmates met the criteria for depression. As for psychotic disorders, about 15% of state inmates and 24% of jail inmates reported symptoms that met criteria (Bureau of Justice Statistics, 2006). Kupers (1999) estimated that 10 to 20 percent of state and federal inmates require serious intensive treatment. A special report from the Bureau of Justice Statistics, titled *Mental Health Problems of Prison and Jail Inmates* highlighted an alarming situation within our nation's prisons (James & Glaze, 2006, p. 1):

- About 74% of State prisoners and 76% of local jail inmates who had a mental health problem met criteria for substance abuse dependence or abuse.
- Jail inmates who had a mental health problem (24%) were three times as likely as jail inmates without (8%) to report being physically or sexually abused in the past.
- Over 1 in 3 State prisoners and 1 in 6 jail inmates who had a mental health problem had received mental health treatment since admission.
- State prisoners who had a mental health problem were twice as likely as State prisoners without to have been injured in a fight since admission (20% compared to 10%).

EMPLOYERS OF MENTAL HEALTH
COUNSELORS IN CORRECTIONS

In search of employment, job opportunities for master's level mental health counselors are likely to be obtained with state and federal government agencies (Boothby & Clements; 2002; Hawk; 1997; Helwig, 1996; Kupers, 1999; Pallone, 1991). On the federal level, facilities range from penitentiaries to prison camps (Bosworth, 2002). There are approximately 160 prisons and 170,000 inmates housed within the federal system, excluding privately-managed facilities (Bureau of Federal Prisons, 2009). Similarly, state facilities cover a range of settings as well, including maximum-security prisons, detention centers, and boot camps. Such facilities are operated by the state's respective Department of Corrections (DOC). Master's level mental health professionals should note that correctional agencies job opportunities may vary from state to state, and even within states. For example, some states, such as the California Department of Corrections and Rehabilitation, require their psychologist to be licensed-eligible. Yet, in the State of Maryland—Department of Corrections, individuals are hired as psychology associates at the master's degree level without the need for a license. However, there is greater potential to be hired within state or privately-managed facilities at the master's degree level, in comparison to the federal system. The Federal Bureau of Prisons on the other hand tends to mostly hire licensed-eligible doctoral holders (Boothby & Clements, 2002).

In addition to state and federal agencies, the advent of private prisons has emerged as major employers of mental health professionals. Private prisons are contracted by governments to operate correctional facilities. According to the Bureau of Justice Statistics (2000), there were fourteen companies operating 153 private prisons in the United States. Private prisons are located in 31 states across the country. In 2005, as the largest of these contractors, Corrections Corporation of American (CCA) had 63 facilities in 19 states and the District of Columbia (cited in Lynch, 2007). CCA housed 55 percent of all inmates in private prisons, culminating in over 67,000 inmates. For further information, please refer to http://correctionscorp.com.

JOB DESCRIPTION AND RESPONSIBILITIES

As integral members of the correctional staff, the primary role and responsibility of mental health professionals is to promote and maintain a healthy (prison) environment for staff and inmates alike (Hawk, 1997). More specifically, counselors provide direct mental health services to offenders, including psychological screenings, crisis intervention, individual and group counseling, and the development of programs and activities. The foci of such services may vary among institutions. For example, depending on the security level of the facility (e.g., pretrial, maximum, or pre-release), counselors may devote more time providing one service over another. According to a national survey among master's and doctoral level psychologists, respondents reported the following with respect to time engaged in responsibilities: administrative task (30%); direct treatment (26%); assessment (18%); crisis intervention (9%); staff training (8%); consultation (7%); and research (1%) (Boothby & Clements, 2002).

Assessment. Upon admission, many inmates require a psychological screening, evaluation, and/ or assessment (Bonta, Cormier, Peters, Gendreau, & Marwuis, 1983; Hawk 1997; Morgan, 2003: Weinstein, Kim, Mack, Malavade, & Saraiya, 2005). The results of evaluations are typically used by prison administration, review committees and boards, and other personnel to assist with making decisions regarding a particular inmate. In some instances, assessment services are mandated by the court system. Further, upon intake, psychological evaluations are useful in determining which inmates will require ongoing mental health services. Psychological evaluations are also warranted when inmates change security level (e.g., from minimum to pre-release). In completing the evaluations, counselors usually gather information from three primary sources: (a) clinical interview with the inmate; (b) clinical and case management file; and (c) psychometric assessment (Bonta et al, 1983). Therefore, potential employees (e.g., mental health counselors) are required to possess competent skills in assessment administration, scoring, interpreting, and report writing. Bonta and colleagues (1983, p. 136) listed several reasons or questions that may warrant the referral of a psychological evaluation:

- Does this inmate require segregation for his own safety or that of others?
- Is a psychiatric referral appropriate for this case?
- Is this inmate likely to function well in the minimum security wing of the detention centre?
- Is this inmate likely to honor a temporary absence pass?
- Is this inmate a good candidate for placement in a community residential centre?
- In considering this inmate's transfer to a correctional setting, what security level is most appropriate?
- What specific treatment program does he/she require while incarcerated, and is he/she likely to benefit from such a program?
- Are there service agencies in the community to which he/she should be referred upon release?

Crisis Intervention. While incarcerated, a large number of inmates experience emotional or behavioral instability (e.g., anxiety, depression, and stress) that would warrant crisis intervention services (Morgan, 2003). There are a plethora of reasons for crisis intervention referrals, such as difficulty managing conflict with other inmates, coping with urgent family matters (e.g., death in family), and ambiguity surrounding legal status. Not to mention, obviously, adjusting to the prison environment and conditions can be especially traumatic, distressful, and fretful. Particularly upon first entering prison, feelings of shame, fear, and anguish can be debilitating (Bonta et al., 1983; Boothby & Clements, 2002; Konrad, Daigle, Daniel, Dear, Frottier, Hayes, Kerkhof, Liebling, & Sarchiapone, 2007). The culmination of being alienated from "love ones," harassment from other inmates, and uncertainty regarding the future, may lead to suicidal thoughts or behaviors.

Konrad et al., (2007) contended that, "suicide is often the single most common cause of death in correctional settings" (p. 113). In comparison to the general population, inmates have higher suicide rates (Hayes, 2005; Konrad et al., 2007; Morgan, 2003). As the leading cause of death is jails across the United States, more than 400 inmates commit suicide each year, which is five times higher than the general population rate (Hayes, 2005). Given the high probability of suicide within correctional facilities, counselors must be extremely cautious, vigilant, and cognizant in preventing such an occurrence. In doing so, Konrad and colleagues (2007) identified several common profile factors among suicide inmates that may be useful in the development of suicide screening and prevention programs: (a) situational factors (e.g., segregation); (b) psychosocial factors (e.g., poor social support); (c) women; and (d) juveniles. Once the inmate has been deemed "at risk," counselors must proceed diligently in implementing safeguards (e.g., observation room/ unit) to prevent against self-injury or harm. Since most suicide attempts occur, during times, outside the purview of the mental health professional, correctional staff must be appropriately trained to prevent, manage, and intervene during these instances. As such, it is the role and responsibility of mental health professionals to provide training to correctional staff.

Individual Counseling. Depending on the type of facility, it is fairly common for mentally ill inmates to seek ongoing counseling treatment. Counseling sessions may be short (1–3 sessions) or long term (3–6 months) in nature; in any case, the mental health counselor may develop a caseload. Treatment would involve addressing a host of pathologies, such as psychotic disorders, mood disorders, personality disorders, and anxiety disorders (Fagan & Ax, 2003). Many of these inmates may have received treatment prior to incarceration and wish to continue while detained. These individuals are also likely to have been prescribed psychotropic medications. In most instances, inmates are referred by staff members who are concerned about the inmates' mental health status (Bonta et al., 1983). For inmates who exhibit behavior problems or "acting out," mental health professionals may be required to develop a behavior treatment plan (Bonta et al., 1983).

In addition to those who enter prison or jail with preexisting mental health problems, there are many inmates who develop neurosis as a result of confinement (Kupers, 1996; Pallone, 1991). As alluded to previously, the experiences and conditions in prisons and jails, for many inmates, are unbearable. It is difficult maintaining normality given the abnormality of the environment. For example, the experience of not seeing or talking with "love ones" is especially traumatic for female inmates (Kupers, 1996). Kupers (1996) maintains that women who have minimum contact with their children; subsequently, experience profound emotional distress. In situations, whereas, the female is a single-mother (70%), the children may be taken into foster care. Such experiences tend to foster a deep depression and anxiety in women (Kupers, 1996). As a mental health counselor, it is extremely important to be aware of and sensitive to gender-specific needs of female inmates. Given the prevalence of the above example, it would be ideal to develop therapeutic groups and/ or programs to assist women in coping with these traumatic experiences.

Rape is another traumatic experience that may cause an inmate to seek individual counseling. Data from the Federal Bureau of Prisons estimate that between 9 and 20 percent of male inmates have been sexually victimized while incarcerated (as cited in Kupers, 1996). Undoubtedly, these estimates are conservative, given the fact that a substantial number of these cases are unreported. With respect to women, a majority of the perpetrators are male staff. The psychological severity of such an experience is likely to promote onset symptoms of posttraumatic stress disorder. Moreover, Kupers (1996) noted that female inmates are likely to have been raped or sexually abused as children, whereby they relive past trauma when they are retraumatised in a prison. Following rape, symptoms that may occur include flash-backs, nightmares, hyperarousal, startle, hypervigilance, and panic. Other symptoms, such as social isolation, curtailing of activities, and withdrawal are likely occurrences.

Group Counseling and Programs. Mental health professionals are also responsible for developing and implementing psychoeducational groups, programs, and other activities. Most groups focus on a particular segment of the population or topic area, such as anger management, stress management, sexual offenders, and substance abuse. Given the significant increase in prison population and subsequent greater need to provide mental health services to more inmates, group counseling has become a widely used intervention (Morgan, Winterowd, & Ferrell, 1999). One important benefit of group counseling is that it allows inmates to socialize and create interpersonal relationships that would otherwise be non-existent. By connecting with others, social support networks are established and useful in coping with the reality of incarceration. Another benefit is that group counseling provides the opportunity for inmates to experience therapeutic psychodynamics, such as universality, group cohesiveness, and altruism (cited in Morgan, Winterowd, & Ferrell, 1999). However, there are several limitations to group counseling in a correctional setting. For example, confidentiality is not necessarily guaranteed, which may curtail authentic catharses. In fact, breach of confidentiality could possible spiral out of control and create a potentially dangerous situation.

In addition to group counseling, facilitating group programs and activities are primary responsibilities of mental health professionals in prisons as well. In recent years, there has been an increase in treatment programs designed for inmates with dual diagnosis (e.g., mental health disorder and substance use). An estimated 3% to 11% of jail and prison inmates have a dual diagnosis (Peters & Matthews, 2003). The demand for dual diagnosis programs continues to grow as "tougher" drug laws have increased drug convictions and sentencing. This increase in "tougher laws" is in spite of clear evidence that prevention and education of substance abusers is far more effective than incarceration in prisons (NIDA, 2009). From 1980 to 2004, drug offenders in state and federal prisons increased from 25,000 to over 330,000. A national survey on state prisoners revealed that nearly 75% of inmates are in need of substance abuse treatment. These specialized programs focus on the collaboration among law enforcement, mental health, and substance abuse. According to Peters and Matthews (2003, p. 89), these programs typically use a modified therapeutic community approach; whereby, there is extended involvement in treatment, emphasis on psychoeducation, shorter duration of treatment sessions, smaller client caseload, less confrontation, and more individual support to include counseling activities.

EDUCATION AND TRAINING

For master's level mental health professionals, pursuing a career in corrections has become widespread. According to federal law, prison inmates have a constitutional right to mental health treatment (Cohen & Gerbasi, 2005). As such, most facilities have, at minimum, one licensed doctoral-level psychologist (Ph.D. or Psy.D.) on staff. However, at the master's level, there are no requirements to be certified or licensed as a counselor. Rather, these individuals must practice under the clinical supervision of a licensed doctoral level psychologist. They are usually referred to as psychology associates. The role and responsibilities of the psychology associate are primarily no different from their superiors, with the exception of supervision as a responsibility. According to the research, within state correctional facilities, master's level counselors are employed at the same rate as doctoral psychologist (Magaletta & Boothby, 2003). In most states, potential employees must hold a master's degree from an accredited program in psychology, counseling, social work, or a social science-related discipline.

With respect to training, research suggest that mental health counselors who had prior training experience with offenders, as an intern, reported higher level of job satisfaction (Boothby & Clements, 2002). Therefore, it would behoove potential employers to seek a practicum or internship experience at a correctional facility prior to seeking employment. As stated previously, there are a number of correctional facilities that offer opportunities for students to receive clinical training (Boothby & Clements, 2002). Additionally, it would be beneficial to have taken courses related to the job description, such as:

- Advanced Techniques in Counseling
- Group Dynamics
- Psychological Assessment
- Drug and Alcohol Counseling
- Personality Theory
- Diagnosis and Psychopathology
- Career Counseling

- Psychopharmacology
- Multicultural Counseling

PERSONAL CHARACTERISTICS OF MENTAL HEALTH COUNSELOR

Unlike other settings where mental health counselors are employed, correctional facilities are perhaps deemed as the most dangerous in terms of personal safety. However, contrary to popular belief, Boothby and Clements (2002) noted that correctional psychologists rated safety among the most satisfying regarding job satisfaction. Still, in working with criminals and offenders, it recommended and required that mental health counselors remain highly vigilant, incisive, and confident. Unsurprisingly, prison inmates are also among the most deceitful in their self-presentation (Benedict & Lanyon, 1992); therefore, mental health counselors must avoid being easily vulnerable to manipulation and persuasiveness (Helwig, 1996). Counselors should also possess confrontation skills, even-temperedness, and objectivity to problems shared by the inmates. Particularly, with respect to antisocial inmates (e.g., sexual offenders, rapists, and the like), counselors must continue to demonstrate tact, patience, and professional integrity in order to successfully provide services. Needless to say, correctional facilities are among the most stimulating, challenging, and demanding environments to work. Yet, it is also extremely rewarding!

SUMMARY

To conclude, the author has, personally, had many humbling experiences while working within the correctional counseling milieu. Within corrections, mental health professionals are responsible for delivering a host of services, including psychological assessments, crisis intervention, individual counseling, group counseling and programs. Given the recent rise in inmates with mental illness, correctional systems are in constant need of recruiting mental health professionals (Boothby & Clements,

2002). Regardless of the reasons, whether "tougher" drug policies or the closing of mental health hospitals, America's correctional facilities are replete with mentally ill inmates. In response, the federal courts have mandated upgrades in mental health services (e.g., *Coleman v. Wilson, 1985; Ruiz v. Estelle, 1980*), which has subsequently led to the massive recruitment in the field. For master's level mental health counselors in particular, the field of corrections is a very promising one!

REFERENCES

Alexander, E. (2000). The care and feeding of the correctional-industrial complex. In J. P. Mays & K. R. Pitts (Eds*), Building violence: How America's rush to incarcerate creates more violence* (pp. 51–55). Thousand Oaks: Sage Publications, Inc.

Benedict, L.W. Lanyon, R.I. (1992). An analysis of deceptiveness: Incarcerated prisoners. *Journal of Addictions and Offender Counseling, 13*, 23–31.

Bonta, J., Cormier, R., Peters, R.D., Gendreau, P., & Marquis, H. (1983). Psychological servicesin jails. *Canadian Psychology, 24:2*, 135–139.

Boothby, J.L. & Clements, C.B. (2002). Job satisfaction of correctional psychologists: Implications for recruitment and retention. *Professional Psychology: Research and Practice, 22*, 310–315.

Bosworth, M. (2002). *The U.S. federal prison system*. Thousand Oaks: Sage Publications.

Bureau of Federal Prisons. (2009). Weekly Population Report. Retrieved April 17, 2008 from U.S. Department of Justice. Web site: http://www.bop.gov/locations/weekly_report.jsp.

Bureau of Justice Statistics. (2008). Retrieved April 17, 2008 from Office of Justice Programs: U.S. Department of Justice. Web site: http://www.ojp.usdoj.gov/bjs/correct.htm.

Cohen, F. & Gerbasi, J.B. (2005). Legal issues regarding the provision of mental health care in correctional settings. In C.L. Scott & J.B. Gerbasi (Eds.), *Handbook of correctional mental health* (pp. 259–284). Washington, DC: American Psychiatric Publishing, Inc.

Fagan, T.J. (2003). Mental health in corrections. In T.J. Fagan & R.K. Ax (Eds.), *Correctional mental health handbook* (pp. 1–16). Thousand Oaks: Sage Publications.

Fagan, T.J. & Ax, R.K. (2003). *Correctional mental health handbook*. Thousand Oaks: Sage Publications.

Hamlett, M.A., (2006). *A critical race perspective: Private prisons in American*. Urbana, IL: University of Illinois Press.

Hawk, K.M. (1997). Personal reflections on a career in correctional psychology. *Professional Psychology: Research and Practice, 28*, 335–337.

Hayes, L.M., (2005). Suicide prevention in correctional facilities. In C.L. Scott & J.B. Gerbasi (Eds.), *Handbook of correctional mental health* (pp. 69–88). Washington, DC: American Psychiatric Publishing, Inc.

Helwig, A.A. (1996). Careers in federal and state agencies. In B.B. Collison & N.J. Garfield (Eds.) *Careers in counseling and human services, 2nd Edition* (pp. 73–93). Washington, DC: Taylor & Francis.

Institute of Medicine. (2007). *Ethical considerations for research involving prisoners*. Washington, DC: The National Academics Press.

James, D.J. & Glaze, L.E. (2006). *Mental health problems of prison and inmates, 2006*. Bureau of Justice Statistics. Washington, DC: U.S. Department of Justice.

Konrad, N., Daigle, M.S., Daniel, A.E., Dear, G.E., Frottier, P., Hayes, L.M., Kerkof, A., Liebling, A., & Sarchiapone, M. (2007). Preventing suicide in prisons, Part I: Recommendations from the international association for suicide prevention task force on suicide in prisons. *Crisis, 28*, 113–121.

Kupers, T. (1999). *Prison madness: The mental health crisis behind bars and what we must do about it*. San Francisco: Jossey-Bass Publishers.

Lynch, M.J. (2007). *Big prisons big dreams: Crime and the failure of America's penal system*. New Jersey: Rutgers University Press.

Magaletta, P. & Boothby, J. (2003). Correctional mental health professionals. In T.J. Fagan &R.K. Ax (Eds.), *Correctional mental health handbook* (pp. 21–54). Thousand Oaks: Sage Publications.

Morgan, R. (2003). Basic mental health services: Services and issues. In T.J. Fagan & R.K. Ax(Eds.), *Correctional mental health handbook* (pp. 57–69). Thousand Oaks: Sage Publications.

Morgan, R.D., Winterwood, C.L., & Ferrell, S.W. (1999). A national survey of group psychotherapy services in correctional facilities. *Professional Psychology: Research and Practice, 30*, 600–606.

National Institute on Drug Abuse. (1999). *Thirteen principles of effective drug addiction treatment.* NIDA Notes. Vol. 14, Number 5, December.

Pallone, N.J. (1991). *Mental disorder among prisoners: Toward an epidemiologic inventory.* New Brunswick: Transaction Publishers.

Peters, R.H. & Matthews, C.O. (2003). Substance abuse treatment. In T.J. Fagan & R.K. Ax (Eds.), *Correctional mental health handbook* (pp. 73–94). Thousand Oaks: Sage Publications.

Reese, R. (2006). *Prison race.* Durham, NC: Carolina Academic Press.

Scott, C.L. & Gerbasi, J.B. (2005). *Handbook of correctional mental health.* Washington, DC:American Psychiatric Publishing, Inc.

VanderWaal, C.J., Taxman, F.S., & Gurka-Ndanyi, M.A. (2008). Reforming drug treatment services to offenders: Cross-system collaboration, integrated policies, and a seamless continuum of care model. *Journal of Social Work Practice in the Addictions, 8(1),* 127–153.

Weinstein, H.C., Kim, D., Mack, A.H., Malavade, K.E., & Saraiya, A.U. (2005). Prevalence and assessment of mental disorders in correctional settings. In C.L. Scott & J.B. Gerbasi (Eds.), *Handbook of correctional mental health* (pp. 43–68). Washington, DC: American Psychiatric Publishing, Inc.

Wood, P.J. (2003). The rise of the prison industrial complex in the United States. In A. Coyle, A. Campbell, & R. Neufeld (Eds.), *Capitalist punishment: Prison privatization & human rights* (pp. 16–29). Atlanta, GA: Clarity Press, Inc.

Section Two

Working with Families

The Family Counselor/Therapist

7

By Rosalyn Greene, Ph.D.

This chapter is designed for people who seek to (1) help families and couples with their relationships; (2) change something about society that is interconnected with relationships; and (3) help individuals with behavioral, emotional, vocational, social, educational, physical, and spiritual issues that are somehow interconnected with their relationships. As a family counselor/therapist there is the expectancy that help, services, expertise, and support will be given to those who are not functioning to their full potential. Respect, caring, and competence are terms implied in the care-giving.

INTRODUCTION

Relationships have the potential to bring out the best and the worst in people. The family counselor/therapist job is to help challenge and support individuals in ways to help them move past the limitations in their relationships. A relationship between the counselor/therapist and the client should be one that allows the client to feel as though he/she can open up and discover themselves and become more like their ideal selves.

Family counseling/therapy teaches us that the family is more than a collection of separate individuals; it is a system, an organic whole whose parts function and rely on the interconnectedness and interactions of each other rather than separate beings. But even as members of family systems, family members do not cease being individuals with hearts, minds, and wills, of their own. Although it is impossible to understand people without taking into account their social environment, it is misleading to limit the focus solely to the surface of interactions. Working with the family system means considering all the members of the family, and the personal dimensions of their experience within their family.

Choosing to work with families and couples is a life-altering choice. Family counseling/therapy is extremely personal work that can be quite hard to leave at the office. The emotional challenges and rewards can be intense. In addition to the cognitive and interactional skills, professionals must confront echoes and similarities of their current relationships and their own family of origin. Personally, counselors/therapists must manage the anxiety of not knowing a solution to a problem and they must also cope with the responsibility of knowing that whatever they do is likely to have some kind of effect on the family.

BRIEF HISTORY OF FAMILY COUNSELING/THERAPY

Family counseling/therapy is the extension of the attempt by people throughout history to help emotional sufferings. This help took two forms:

1. Elders gave younger members of family clans and tribes advice on interpersonal relationships.
2. Adult members of these social units took care of the very young and the very old (Strong & DeVault, 1998).

Despite this history, family counseling/therapy, with its roots in the 20th century, is one of the newest helping professions. Before 1940, family counseling/therapy in the United States was almost nonexistent. This new helping profession began to grow when women began to enroll in colleges and demanded courses in family life education (Broderick & Schrader, 1981). The second event for the development of family counseling/therapy was the initial establishment of marriage counseling in the late 1920's and 1930's. The third impetus to the rise of family counseling/therapy was the founding of the National Council on Family Relations in 1938 and its journal, *Marriage and Family Living* in 1939. The fourth event that helped to launch family counseling/ therapy was the work of home extension agents such as Alfred Adler who began working with families with his establishment of child care centers (Dinkmeyer, Dinkmeyer & Sperry, 2000; Sherman, 1999).

From 1940 to 1949, family counseling/therapy flourished with the establishment of the American Association of Marriage Counselors (AAMC) formed in 1942. In 1948 the first account of concurrent marital therapy was published. The study of families of schizophrenics was also focused on in the 1940's. Also, last but not least, in the 1940's was World War II and its aftermath. The events of the war brought much stress to millions of families in the United States. These stressors included men separated from families, women working in factories, and death and disabilities of family members.

Some family counselor/therapist historians consider the 1950's as the genesis of the movement. Development of this new profession of working with families was more so during this era because the focus was more on people than on organization. Among the leading per- sonalities during the 1950's were Nathan Ackerman, Gregory Bateson, Carl Whitaker, and Murray Bowen. The decade of the 1960's was an era of rapid growth for family counseling/therapy. The idea of working with families was embraced by prominent figures such as Jay Hayley, Salvador Minuchin, and Virginia Satir. Institutes and training centers also came into prominence in the 1960's.

The 1970's were marked by noted events in regard to family coun- seling/therapy. These events included increased membership in the American Association for Marriage and Family Therapy (AAMFT), the founding of the American Family Therapy Association (AFTA), and the refinement of theories. In the 1980's new leadership emerged in family counseling/therapy—women began to come to the forefront. Membership in the organizations grew, publications increased, and national recognition was given to family counseling/therapy. From 1990 to the present, new theories and specialties within family therapy emerged as well as a growth in family counselors/therapists.

COUNSELING TODAY'S CHANGING *FAMILY*

Society today has become more complex and diverse. The family has and is undergoing dramatic transformation in composition, form, and structure. Americans are living longer, opting to live together prior to marriage, marrying later (if at all), and are divorcing more rapidly.

Today's families are more likely to experience more family transitions during their life span than previous generations (Carlson, Sperry, & Lewis, 1997). The traditional nuclear family in which the man is the sole breadwinner and the woman is the full-time homemaker, wife, and mother is no longer the norm, but a thing of the past. Families led by single parents are becoming commonplace. Cohabitation has replaced marriage for an increasing number of couples. Stepfamilies or blended families make up a major portion of marriages. Gay and lesbian couples are more open in their relationships than in the past. The surge of women in the workplace, the need for two or more incomes to make ends meet, the need to balance work and family responsibilities, concern over proper child care, increased number of children living in poverty, and the rise of single people living alone, are just some of the realities in what Skolnick (1991) states that the North American family is in an "age of uncertainty."

It is not surprising that today's counselors/therapists are faced with clients who present a wide variety of attitudes, complexities, experiences and lifestyles. Likewise, relationship issues have changed. Therefore those in the helping professions must be prepared to think of families, couples, and other combinations of people in terms of how they view themselves and their search for new life paths. The family counselor/therapist must help their clients face difficulties that arise from issues that at one time were less common, such as helping a couple struggling with infertility, or helping a same sex couple work out adoption plans. Another problem might be an example where a counselor/therapist is called upon to help divorce parents where custody is shared, or where one or more children are moving from the father's household to the mother's household every three or four days. Problems may also arise from two or more adults living in an alternative life style. Or conflict may arise between children from two sets of parents joined together in a blended family situation. Counselors/therapists should also be aware of the general stressors inherent in family structures. They need to be more sensitized to the ethnic, racial, and social class backgrounds of clients.

FAMILY RESILIENCY

All families face crisis at some point in their life cycle. The family as a whole, or one or more of its members may manifest dysfunctional behavior during these times of crisis, but that is not to say that the family system is not without strengths or resources. Resilience is the developmental process unique to each family that enables the family system to create adaptive responses to stress, and in some cases even thrive and grow in their response to the stressors. While some families become less functional and even dysfunctional in response to life stressors, some have learned to draw on their internal strengths, which have allowed them to bounce back from adversity. These families are happier, more stable, more competent, and more flexible, show greater recuperative ability, and are more adaptive to changing external conditions (McCubbin, McCubbin, & Thompson, 1993; Hawley & deHaan, 1996).

Resilient families are not free of problems or issues, but have developed the ability to survive and regenerate even in the midst of misfortune, hardships, overwhelming stress and devastating life-altering transitions (the untimely death of a loved one, a sudden job loss, a divorce, the birth of a special needs child). Resiliency is apt to come into play with family members if they do not see themselves as victims, but rather as having a sense of control over their lives. In working with families that are experiencing severe stressors, counselors/therapists must assist the family system in identifying and fortifying the key interactional processes that will help the family to withstand and rebound disruptive challenges (Walsh, 1996). Walsh (1996) believes that the key to family recovery is family resiliency:

How a family confronts and manages a disruptive experience, buffers stress, effectively reorganizes, and moves forward with life will influence immediate and long term adaptation for all family members and for the family unit (p. 267).

COUNSELING THE SINGLE-PARENT-LED FAMILY

Single-parent-led families represent the fastest growing family type in the United States (U.S. Bureau of the Census, 1998). One in four families in the United States represents one-parent family. Whether from separation, divorce, widowhood, out-of-wedlock birth, or adoption, close to 20 million children under the age of 18 live with one parent. It was purported in the late 1980's that 50% to 60% of children born in the 1990's would reside in single family settings (Hetherington, Bridges, & Insabella, 1998). The result of continuing high divorce rate and single women opting to have children have led to the increase of single-parent-led families.

The high rate of marital dissolution has brought about sweeping changes in the contemporary American family. It is a fact that approximately 50% of couples that marry today will eventually end in permanent separation or divorce. The median length of marriage is about seven years (Cox, 1996). A number of individual as well as couple interactive factors can contribute to marital unhappiness. Interpersonal issues that are at the core of marital breakups include:

- Anxiety over making and /or maintaining a long-term commitment
- Inability to respond positively to changing role demands such as those brought about by the return to paid work by a partner or by the birth of a first child.
- Indifference or lack of sensitivity to a partner's wishes or feelings
- Conflicts over independence, children, money, or in-laws
- Fewer shared activities
- Sexual incompatibilities

- Physical abuse
- Infidelity
- Ineffective communication patterns
- Conflicts over control and power
- Reduced exchange of affection
- Underdeveloped problem-solving skills

The counselor/therapist seeing individuals in the process of a marital break-up must be attuned to the blows to self-esteem, depression, hostility, and bitterness that separation and divorce inevitably cause.

In assessing single-parent-led families, the family counselor/therapist needs to explore the following factors:

- How single parenting came about (through never married, desertion, divorce, or death)
- At what time during the marriage did the parent become single (after one year or after 16 years)
- The precipitating factors of the marital break-up (infidelity, immaturity of one or both partners, financial problems irreconcilable differences, sexual incompatibilities, chronic quarreling and dissatisfaction, in-law intrusions)
- The number of children, the age of the children, as well as the age of the custodial parent, and the degree and involvement of extended family members
- The build up of stressor events following a marriage or relationship dissolution and family reorganization (constant fighting between the parents, threats and counterthreats between parents, forcing children to choose sides)
- The changing roles family members have been forced to accept (head of a one-parent household, child takes on more adult responsibilities due to the absence of one parent)
- The role of the absent parent or other significant adults in the current single-parent family system

- The quality of relationships within the nuclear family between the family of origin and the former mates
- The effectiveness of the single parent's resiliency and coping skills, ability to organize and lead the family while adapting to change, sense of mastery
- The single-parent family's relationship with the broader social system (church, legal systems, schools, or welfare)

In addition, counselors/therapists need to be aware that one-parent households led by fathers will probably experience different sets of problems and different lifestyles. They also need to attend to clients' social class as well as their racial and ethnic heritage.

Counselors/therapists in working with single-parent-led families must help them establish boundaries as different family members take on new tasks and responsibilities. They must help them come to terms with the psychological presence of the absent parent. The counselor/therapist may also have to assist the single parent deal with the feelings of depression and eventually the fear of reentering both the social and the work world.

COUNSELING THE REMARRIED FAMILY

Americans enter first marriages at a greater rate than most people in other countries. They also have higher expectations from the marital union and will abandon the relationship if proves unsatisfactory or unfulfilling (Ihinger & Pasley, 1987). One out every three Americans is a stepparent, stepchild, stepsibling, or some member of a stepfamily (Booth & Dunn, 1994). According to Bray (1995), there are more than 11 million remarried families in the United States. Remarriage following divorce has become very familiar to many families in recent years. Although remarriage is not a new phenomenon, its main purpose was to restore the domestic unit and to mend families fragmented by the death of a parent. Presently, remarriage is prevalent following divorce. The blending of two families is a complex and difficult process. The following was observed by Bray (1992):

The structure and membership of stepfamilies create important differences from first married families. These include a lack of socially defined role relationships, problems with defining and maintaining family boundaries, developing affection between new family members, and the challenge of negotiating relationships within the binuclear family system (p. 60).

Remarriage is a complex interactive process over a period of time in which a group of individuals without a common history or a pattern of behaviors attempts to unite and develop a sense of family cohesion and identity. The developmental stages of remarriage are necessary in order to successfully blend two different families. Progression from one stage to the next is easier if the new integrated family has been successful in their completion of the prior stage. The stages outlined below help remarried families better adjust to the new family (Bradt & Bradt, 1986):

1. *Go back:* "Is this a mistake?" "What have I gotten myself into?" "I didn't think it would be like this." The couple may be filled with doubt; the children may attempt to sabotage the relationship; relatives and friends may withhold support.
2. *Making room:* The family members learn to share physical and emotional space with others, avoid the sense of being an intruder, and delineate work and home allocations.
3. *Struggles of realignment:* Power struggles, loyalty conflicts, negotiations and protests occur as former relationship alliances break down and are restructured.
4. *(Re)commitment:* A family identity is established as shared experiences are created and defined, budding family feelings occur, and family ceremonies and rituals are developed.
5. *Rebalancing relationships:* Once recommitment is achieved, the remarried family can easily move back and forth between the old and new households.

6. *Relinquishing feelings of deprivation and burden:* Previously held feelings of isolation, over-responsibilities, untrusting, unwilling to collaborate, hostility, and etc. are given up.

7. *Growth toward integration:* Having accepted differences, relinquished feelings of deprivation, acknowledged complexity, addressed challenges, and established commitments, the family emerges with cohesion and an identity much like any other family.

8. *Moving on:* Members are free to move into more complex relationships outside the family. These relationships focus on problem solving, growth, and interactions with broader systems not within the family.

Working with stepfamilies, the counselor/therapist needs to remember that the remarried pair is part of a larger social system that includes two sets of non-resident parents, children, and an extended family system. Within each family there is a history of issues from previous marital and divorce experiences. As remarried families struggle to develop a family identity they must address some important issues (Ganong, Coleman, & Fine, 1995):

- Developing rules for the new family system
- Deciding what roles will be performed and by whom in the new family
- Establishing a changed hierarchy in the decision making in the new family
- Creating new external boundaries
- Creating new internal boundaries
- Sorting out the larger number of subsystems
- Determining how emotionally cohesive the stepfamily will be

Dealing effectively with the remarried family, the family counselor/therapist will most likely need to help in one or more of the problem areas—mourning for loss, living with differences, resolving loyalty issues, acknowledging the absent parent, living simultaneously in two household, developing a family identity, overcoming boundary issues, and learning co-parenting.

Remarriage is a complex process and in spite of dislocation, it provides an opportunity for family consolidation. Counselors/therapists should always remain aware that remarried families are structurally different from intact biological families with different experiences and traditions. Two very distinct families are attempting to blend into a stable system with an identity of their own.

COUNSELING COHABITATING HETEROSEXUAL ADULTS

"Will you live with me?" appears to have replaced the traditional phrase "Will you marry me?" for a substantial portion of the population. About half of all single people in the United States cohabitate at one time or another before marriage (Saxton, 1996). This living arrangement delays long-term commitment while providing sexual intimacy. Cohabitation means a trial relationship while the couple tests their compatibility before getting married. This alternative lifestyle has become a relatively permanent and recognizable family structure (Bumpass, Raley, & Sweet, 1995). Cohabitation is entered into for a myriad of reasons, many frequently unknown to the partner, despite their stated motives. Counselors/therapists should concern themselves with what sort of individuals choose this living pattern, what motivates them, and why they choose living together rather than marriage. Cohabitating heterosexual adults may experience problems in the following areas:

- Social stigma
- Term for cohabitating partner
- Unequal commitment between partners
- Lack of legal safeguards
- Dealing with families of origin
- Differing views of roles and lifestyles
- Monogamous versus nonmonogamous sexual relationship

- Division of money, labor, and resources
- Parenting of other's children
- Differing views of autonomy
- Differing expectations terminating the relationship

The counselor/therapist's primary goal is to help couples become aware of issues between them and learn some skills for resolving them.

COUNSELING GAY MALE AND LESBIAN FAMILIES

Cohabitating homosexuals have much in common with cohabitating heterosexual adults. Both face some form of ostracism, both are part of a minority system that seek to find intimacy and affectional needs thru unorthodox living arrangements. Both groups contain members of all occupational and socioeconomic groups. Although gay couples have much in common with cohabitating heterosexual adults, they also have some major differences. Homosexual families have a greater rejection by society, have more determined efforts at concealment, and have more self-condemnation. Most gays and lesbians must struggle with achieving self-acceptance in a society in which homosexuality conjures up rejection and negative stereotypes from family, church, and nongay friends. Gay partners may have to deal with the following issues (McWhirter & Mattison, 1982):

- Communication difficulties with feelings between partners causing relationship distress and fatigue
- Their own covert or overt homophobic attitudes leading to low self-esteem and lack of self-acceptance.
- The brevity of role models for their relationship which can lead to uncertainty or the adoption of inappropriate male-female behaviors
- The degree to which as individuals and as a couple they are open with gay and nongay friends, family, employees, and colleagues.

Gay couples rarely come to counseling to change their sexual orientation, but rather to deal with relationship issues much like those of nongay couples. In counseling gay couples, it is important for counselors/therapists to consider the impact of the HIV/AIDS epidemic on the gay population. Counseling intervention usually takes one of two forms: pre-AIDS test counseling and posttest counseling. In the pretest counseling, the focus is on helping gay clients explore the degree of risk in their sexual behavior patterns. Since testing is a crucial part of the pre-AIDS counseling that can lead to depression, lack of sleep, and even suicidal thoughts, counselors/therapists must limit their input regarding testing, although giving accurate and up-to-date information about the test. In general, posttest counseling is helping those infected with the HIV virus. Counseling gays who test positive for the HIV virus or with full blown AIDS involves helping them deal with fears of loss of independence, rejection of a lover, punishment by society for being gay, financial problems, disclosure of their homosexuality to family and friends, becoming physically helpless, the infection of partners, and their own ultimate death.

COUNSELING THE DUAL-CAREER FAMILY

Dual-earner families are not a new phenomenon in the United States. Over the last several decades a significant amount of women have entered the workforce (Cox, 1996). These families are the most common style family in society. In such arrangements both partners are employed for pay with the wife working outside the home for one or more of the following reasons: because the family needs her income for economic survival, because her paycheck enhances the family's standard of living, or because she finds working away from home fulfilling and gratifying. Work-family conflicts are normally present when dual wage earners work a combined 80 hours for the week. At the center of every dual-career marriage is an attempt to redefine the relationship between family and work. Achieving a balance between the two is never an easy task for any couple. In reality making a two-career marriage work requires the ability for couples to challenge the traditional views about the rights and roles of men and women in our society. Tension often ensues as each spouse takes on tasks that are ordinarily associated with the opposite sex. Flexibility in learning and defining new roles in accommodating family role changes are essential elements in making a dual-career relationship work. Interpersonal conflict and family tension can result in issues around the following:

- Who controls the money? Are there separate or joint accounts? What are the rights of each partner in the spending of the money?
- Are their differences in income? If so, how do these differences affect the balance of power in the relationship?
- What is the division of labor in the household?
- Will household help be necessary? How much is needed? How is it budgeted?
- If there are children, who will be the primary caretaker? Who will be available in emergencies?
- Whose job can better accommodate special school events, teacher conferences, or childhood illnesses?
- How does the couple deal with gender expectations and competiveness?
- How do they deal with burnout and overload?
- How does the couple allocate their time in order to nourish their relationship?

In counseling families with both partners working, Gilbert (1988) gives five problem areas:

1. Deciding whether or not to have children
2. Managing stress.
3. Matching career expectations, accomplishments and satisfaction between the partners
4. Struggles with role sharing
5. Accommodating aged parents

The counselor/therapist needs to help the dual-career couple under-stand that they are taking on a marriage that may give them a sense of accomplishment, but often the price is guilt over goals not achieved and exhaustion. Exploring what is important to both partners, their values and priorities, and helping the couple to accept their limitations is a valuable role of the family counselor/therapist. In addition, they might also provide consultation to corporations through psychoeducational workshops and training.

COUNSELING ETHNICALLY DIVERSE MINORITY FAMILIES

American society is in a state of change, made up of varying race, multiple ethnic groups, and millions of people migrating here seeking a better life. How counselors/therapists assess, counsel, and commu-nicate with these diverse families is not only seen through their own professional knowledge, but also through their own "cultural filters"—their values, customs, attitudes, religious beliefs and practices, and perceptions that stem from their own cultural backgrounds (Giordano & Carini-Giordano, 1995).

It has been written that all families are the same, and all families are different. If counselors/therapists are going to make effective change with families, then they must try to distinguish among family behav-iors that are universal, cultural specific, transcultural, or idiosyncratic. In other words, counselors/therapists need to be able to tell the differ-ence among those family situations where basic issues reflect human processes that are similar, and those situations where cultural issues are tangential (Falicov, 1988). According to Ramirez (1991), in order for counselors/therapists to be effective, they need to be culturally sensitive as well as be aware of individual diversity when working with ethnic mi-nority clients. Family counselors/therapists who appreciate the cultural relativity of life are likely to adopt a broader perspective and will thus improve their chances of successfully intervening with their families. At the same time, they must never forget how their own ethnic identity, cultural values and assumptions influence the counseling process.

CREDENTIALS AND LICENSING

In the early years of family counseling, most of the pioneers were active in social work, psychology, counseling, or psychiatry. Counselors/therapists working with families were not uniformly supported by their peers. They needed an organization that matched their shared identity. The American Association of Marriage Counselors (AAMC) was founded in the 1970's. Its increased membership with trained family professionals forced it to reorganize and change its name to the American Association for Marriage and Family Therapy (AAMFT). Other family practitioners have continued to identify as counselors, nurses, psychiatrists, addiction counselors, and social workers choosing to work with couples and families. Over time each of the various professions has developed its own subgroup for family specialties such as The International Association for Marriage and Family Counselors (IAMFC) which is a subgroup of the American Counseling Association. American Family Therapy Academy is a subgroup of the group Family process. International Family Therapy Association (IFTA) which publishes the *Journal of Family Psychotherapy* welcomes members at any educational level.

As of 2003, specialized licenses or certificates for couple and family counseling can be obtained throughout the United States. Specific expectations vary, but all require at least a Master's degree with specific family related content and clinical experience. Some laws have been inclusive to include any psychologist, social worker, or pastoral counselor to become a Certified Marriage Counselor without any kind of specialized training. Laws of this kind can weaken public perception of expertise. Presently there is a growing trend for more restrictive laws, requiring not only specialized education, but also supervised clinical experience and a national licensing exam.

SUMMARY

A family is a natural social system that functions with established rules, communication, and has numerous negotiating differences between its members. They display recurring patterns of interactional sequences in which all members participate. Adapting a relationship perspective, family counselors/therapists view that individual behavior is better understood as occurring within a family social system. Gender, cultural background, and social class play decisive roles in behavioral expectations and attitudes. The meanings, understandings, and assumptions a family makes about the world reflect the stories it has created about itself.

Becoming a family counselor/therapist calls for training that focuses on learning a set of therapeutic techniques with a theoretical understanding of how and under what circumstances to use them. Matching and tailoring to client diagnosis, relational conflict or level of functioning can help maximize counseling benefits.

REFERENCES

Booth, A., & Dunn, J. (Eds.). (1994). *Stepfamilies: Who benefits? Who does not?* Hillsdale, NJ: Erlbaum.

Bradt, J. O., & Bradt, C. M. (1986). Resources in remarried families. In M. Karpel (Ed.), *Family resources: The hidden partner in family therapy.* New York: Guilford.

Bray, J. H. (1992). Family relationships and children's adjustment in clinical and non-clinical stepfather families. *Journal of Family Psychology, 6,* 60–68.

Bray, J. H. (1995). Systems-oriented therapy with stepfamilies. In R. H. Mikesell, D. D. Lusterman, & S. H. McDaniel (Eds.), *Integrating family therapy: Handbook of family psychology and systems theory.* Washington, DC: American Psychological Association.

Broderick, C. B., & Schrader, S. S. (1981). The history of professional marriage and family therapy. In S. Gurman & O. P. Kniskern (Eds.), *Handbook of family therapy, 5–38.* New York: Brunner/ Mazel.

Bumpass, L. L., Raley, R. K., & Sweet, J. A. (1995). The changing character of stepfamilies: Implications of cohabitation and nonmarital childbearing. *Demography, 32,* 425–436.

Carlson, J., Sperry, L., & LewiS, J. A. (1997). *Family therapy: Ensuring treatment efficacy.* Pacific Grove, CA: Brooks/Cole.

Cox, F. D. (1996). *Human intimacy: Marriage, the family, and its meaning.* Minneapolis: West.

Dinkmeyer, D. C., Dinkmeyer, D. C., JR., & Sperry, L. (2000). *Adlerian counseling and psychotherapy* (3rd ed.). Upper Saddle River, NJ: Merrill/ Prentice Hall.

Falicov, C. J. (1988). Learning to think culturally. In H. A. Liddle, D. C. Breunlin, & R. C. Schwartz (Eds.), *Handbook of family therapy training and supervision.* New York: Guilford.

Ganong, L. H., Coleman, M., & Fine, M. (1995). Remarriage and stepfamilies. In R. D. Day, K. R. Gilbert, B. H. Settles, & W. E. Burr (Eds.), *Research and theory in family science.* Pacific Grove, CA: Brooks/ Cole.

Giordano, J., & Carini-Giordano, M. A. (1995). Ethnic dimensions in family treatment. In R. H. Mikesell, D. D. Lusterman, & S. H. McDaniel (Eds.), *Integrating family therapy: Handbook of family psychology and systems theory.* Washington, DC: American Psychological Association.

Hawley, D. R. & De Haan, L. (1996). Toward a definition of family resilience: Integrating life-span and family perspectives. *Family process, 35,* 283–298.

Hetherington, E. M., Bridges, M., & Insabella, G. M. (1998). What matters? What does not? Five perspectives on the association between marital transitions and children's adjustments. *American Psychologist, 53,* 167–184.

Iginger-Tallman, M. & Pasley, K. (1987). Divorce and remarriage in the American family: A historical review. In K. Pasley & M. Ihinger-Tallman (Eds.), *Remarriage and stepparenting: Current research and theory.* New York: Guilford.

Mccubbin, H. I., Mccubbin, M. A., & Thompson, A. I. (1993). Resiliency in families: The role of family schema and appraisal in family adaptation to crises. In T. H. Brubaker (Ed.), *Family relations: Challenges for the future.* Newbury Park, CA: Sage.

Mcwhirter, D. R., & Mattison, A. M. (1982). Psychotherapy for gay couples. In J. C. Gonsiorek (Ed.), *Homosexuality and psychotherapy.* New York: Haworth.

Ramirez, M., III. (1991). *Psychotherapy and counseling with minorities: A cognitive approach to individual and cultural differences.* Boston: Allyn & Bacon.

Saxton, L. (1996). *The individual, marriage, and the family* (9th ed.). Belmont, CA: Wadsworth.

Skolnick, A. (1991). *Embattled paradise: The American family in an age of uncertainty.* New York: Basic.

Strong, B., & DeVault, C. (1998). *The marriage and family experience* (7th ed.). Belmont, CA: Wadsworth.

Walsh, F. (1996). The concept of family resilience: Crisis and challenge. *Family Process, 35,* 261–281.

The Structure of a Family Education Center

8

By Cubie Bragg, Ph.D.

INTRODUCTION

Many students express the desire to establish their own family centers to address the needs of the family. Oftentimes, these students seek the long route in determining how to structure a center. This chapter will provide a structure that can be followed by master level students and provide information about services offered.

Family Education Centers provide an environment to promote an understanding of negative family relationships, values, and practices. This is accomplished by use of individual, group, and or family counseling utilizing an integrated, eclectic approach. Once these factors are recognized, a holistic approach is developed to enhance better cooperation and communication. This approach to treating the family members is supported by the well established understanding that the family relationship can have positive or negative impact on child development (Rutter, 2002).

Children and adolescents can not effectively benefit from treatment without parental support, consent, reimbursement, and transportation (Weisz, Doneberg, Han, Kauneckis, 1995). It has been noted that psychoeducational or cognitive-behavioral treatments have limited applicability with children, who often lack the cognitive capacity to engage in treatments without parental help (Freeman, Garcia, Fucci, Karitani, Miller, Leonard, 2003).

Family Education Centers offer family counseling, couples counseling, anger and classroom management groups, as well as education services for parents, teachers, and child and youth care workers. They offer marriage education, self esteem building sessions, and sessions to teach parents how to develop family meetings. In addition, they provide an environment for children of all ages to interact for groups and other activities which are purposed to foster healthy interpersonal interactions. Family Education Centers also provide an excellent opportunity for Master's level counseling students to begin, develop, and refine their skills as mental health practitioners.

Many Family Education Centers have a specialized focus. For example, Adlerian Family Education Centers provides training and specialization using the Adlerian approach to counseling. The Adlerian Family Education Centers offer an opportunity for students to participate in a part of the family counseling sessions as a training tool. Students may observe interactions in the center that provide an understanding of how children interact with adults who are not their parents and other children who are not their siblings. They observe relationships that are encouraging and others that may be discouraging. It is through these training experiences that Master's level counseling students have the opportunity to learn that these interpersonal interactional patters become very useful for treatment planning. Special focus centers such as these are able to train Master's level counseling students who require supervised experience in the use of a special treatment approach. Most centers are involved in receiving grant funding, therefore, providing students with opportunities to participate in research.

The Adlerian Family Education Center was started by Alfred Adler. Alder believed that children needed a balance of structure and choice, as well as an understanding about the importance of cooperation. Adler began by forming groups of teachers, counselors, and child care workers who he trained to used the Adlerian model. These groups grew to form other family education centers which were located in the state schools of Vienna, Austria. The essential educational purpose of the centers was to provide a place where family members and teachers could learn the principles of social equality, cooperation and mutual respect (McDonough, 2003).

DESIGN AND ESTABLISHMENT OF A FAMILY EDUCATION CENTER
Recommended Guidelines

1. **Develop a mission statement**

   The first step in designing and establishing a Family Education is to develop a realistic mission statement. Clearly state the mission of the Family Education Center. The mission should include the nature and scope of services to be provided. For example, one should consider if the center will service a large diverse population or a special population, such as children with emotional problems.

2. **Develop the "Articles of Incorporation" of the Family Education Center**

   The filing status of the center should be determined. The decision to choose profit or nonprofit has tax implications; therefore, one should check state and federal tax regulations. Most centers are non profit, for tax advantages.

3. **Decide on an Appropriate Name for the Center**

   The name can be the name of the principle owner or a name related to the center's mission and purpose

4. **Decide on Location and Address**

5. **State Specific Purposes for the Center**

   Some examples are:

   - To encourage and support the education of special disadvantaged children and adolescents through educational services and counseling.
   - To promote understanding and advocacy for children and their families with emotional, behavioral, developmental and

learning disorders that may interfere with their educational, social and vocational development.

• To conduct action research that will seek to find practical solutions, helpful interventions and effective instructional paradigms that will help improve the educational, social and vocational outcomes of clinically at risk clients.

DEVELOPMENT OF A BOARD OF DIRECTORS

The recommendation for the board of directors is that the number of board members be between four and seven directors.

The recommended titles are:

• President
• Vice President
• Treasurer
• Secretary

Directors at Large (These positions should be special needed individuals such as Business Manager, Psychiatric Advisor, Clinical Director).

Directors

The center's four to seven directors collectively are known as the Board of Directors.

General Qualifications of Board Members

Directors should be of the age of majority in their location. Other qualifications for directors of the center should be as follows:

1. All directors must be clear and remain clear of any criminal charges beyond misdemeanors and traffic violations;
2. All directors must remain drug free of any drug use.

Powers

Detail the person or persons responsible for the control of the center (the board, CEO or President).

Duties

Duties of the directors may include:

a. Perform any and all duties required of them collectively or individually by law, the Articles of Incorporation, or Bylaws;
b. Vote to appoint and remove, employ and discharge, and, except as otherwise provided the Bylaws, prescribe the duties and fix the compensation, if any, of all officers, agents and employees of the corporation;
c. Review the performance and effectiveness of all officers, agents and employees of the center to assure that their duties are performed properly;
d. Meet at such times and places as required by the Bylaws;
e. Register their addresses with the Secretary of the center, and notices of meetings mailed or e-mail to them at such addresses.

Compensation

Directors should serve without compensation except that a reasonable fee may be paid to directors for attending regular and special meetings of the board. In addition, they should be allowed reasonable advancement or reimbursements of expenses incurred.

Each board member should have special qualifications.

Term of Office

Four board directors should hold office for a period of three years and three board directors should hold office two years so as to preserve continuity by staggering elections.

Note: The period of duration of the Family Education Center. It is recommended that the duration of the center be perpetual.

Vacancies

Vacancies on the Board of Directors:

1.   On the death, resignation or removal of any director, and
2.   whenever the number of authorized directors is increased.

Any director may resign effective upon giving written notice to the Chairperson of the Board, the President, the Secretary, or the Board of Directors, unless the notice specifies a later time for the effectiveness of such resignation. Directors may be removed from office, with or without cause, as permitted by and in accordance with the laws of that location.

Unless otherwise prohibited by the Articles of Incorporation, the Bylaws or provisions of law, vacancies on the board may be filled by approval of the board of directors. If the number of directors then in office is less than a quorum, a vacancy on the board may be filled by approval of a majority of directors then in office or by a sole remaining director. A person elected to fill a vacancy on the board should hold office until the next election of the Board of Directors or until his or her death, resignation or removal from office.

Classes of Membership

1.   **List and Define all Classes of Membership and the Responsibilities of each Membership Group**
     Note any cost for membership.

2.   **List All Benefits and Services Related to Membership**

3.   **List What Happens if the Center Is Dissolved**
     What happens to its assets, debts, and liabilities?

Development/Establishment of Bylaws

1. **Principal Office**

   List location. County or state and country.

2. **Policy for Change of Address for Principal Office**

   Note that the board may change the principal office from one location to another within a particular area by noting the changed address and an effective date.

3. **Other Offices**

   The Center may also provide services and have offices at various locations, within or without its location incorporation, where it is qualified to do business. Clearly state who can approve the services and office locations; is it the owner of the center, its president or board of directors?

Meetings

1. **Place of Meetings**

   Meetings should be held at the principal office of the center unless otherwise provided by the board or at such other place as may be designated from time to time by resolution of the Board of Directors.

2. **Regular Meetings**

   List day, time and all scheduled meetings, noting exceptions (legal holidays, or any other special days that might prevent regular meetings).

3. **Special Meetings**

   Special meetings of the Board of Directors may be called by the Chairperson of the Board, the President, the Vice-President, the Secretary, by any two directors, or, if different, by the persons specifically authorized under the laws of this state to call special meetings of the board. Such meetings should also be held at the principal office of the center, or, if different, at the place designated by the person or persons calling the special meeting.

4. **Notice of Meetings**
    a. <u>Regular Meetings</u>. No notice need be given of any regular meeting of the board of directors.
    b. <u>Special Meetings</u>. At least one week prior notice should be given by the Secretary of the center to each director of each special meeting of the board. Such notice may be oral or written, may be given personally, by first class mail, by telephone, or by facsimile machine, and should state the place, date and time of the meeting and the matters proposed to be acted upon at the meeting. In the case of facsimile notification, the director to be contacted should acknowledge personal receipt of the facsimile notice by a return message or telephone within twenty four hours of the first facsimile transmission.

5. **Quorum for Meetings**
    A quorum should consist of <u>five</u> of the members of the Board of Directors.

    Except as otherwise provided under the Articles of Incorporation, Bylaws, or provisions of law, no business should be considered by the board at any meeting at which the required quorum is not present, and the only motion which the Chair should entertain at such meeting is a motion to adjourn.

6. **Board Actions During meetings**
    Every act or decision done or made by a majority of the directors present at a meeting duly held at which a quorum is present is the act of the Board of Directors, unless the

Articles of Incorporation, Bylaws, or provisions of law require a greater percentage or different voting rules for approval of a matter by the board.

7.   **Conduct of Meetings**
     Meetings of the Board of Directors should be presided over by the Chairperson or President of the Board, or, if no such person has been so designated or, in his or her absence, the President of the center or, in his or her absence, by the Vice President of the center or, in the absence of each of these persons, by a Chairperson chosen by a majority of the directors present at the meeting. The Secretary of the center should act as secretary of all meetings of the board, provided that, in his or her absence, the presiding officer should appoint another person to act as Secretary of the Meeting.

     Meetings should be governed by established rules of orders, insofar as such rules are not inconsistent with or in conflict with the Articles of Incorporation, the Bylaws, or with provision of law.

Nonliability of Directors

The directors should not be personally liable for the debts, liabilities, or other obligations of the center.

Indemnification by Corporation of Directors and Officers

The directors and officers of the center should be indemnified by the center to the fullest extent permissible under the law of your location.

Insurance for Corporate Agents

Except as may be otherwise provided under provisions of law, the Board of Directors may adopt a resolution authorizing the purchase and maintenance of insurance on behalf of any agent of the center (including a director, officer, employee or other agent of the center) against liabilities asserted against or insured by the agent in such capacity or arising out of the agent's status as such, whether or not the center would have the power to indemnify the agent against such liability under the Articles of Incorporation, the Bylaws or provisions of law.

OFFICERS
Designation of Officers

The officers of the center should be a President, a Vice President, a Secretary, and a Treasurer. The center may also have a Chairperson of the Board, one or more Vice Presidents, Assistant Secretaries, Assistant Treasurers, and other such officers with such titles as may be determined from time to time by the Board of Directors.

Qualifications

Officers should be of the age of majority of your location. Other qualifications for officers of this corporation should be as follows:

1. All directors must be clear and remain clear of any criminal charges beyond misdemeanors and traffic violations.
2. All directors must remain drug free and may not perform any of the organization's duties while impaired under the influence of alcohol. Any person may serve as officer of this corporation.

Election and Term of Office

Officers should be elected by the Board of Directors, at any time, and each officer should hold office until he or she resigns or is removed or is otherwise disqualified to serve, or until his or her successor should be elected and qualified, whichever occurs first.

Removal and Resignation

Any officer may be removed, either with or without cause, by the Board of Directors, at any time. Any officer may resign at any time by giving written notice to the Board of Directors or to the President or Secretary of the center. Any such resignation should take effect at the date of receipt of such notice or at any later date.

Vacancies

Any vacancy caused by the death, resignation, removal, disqualification, or otherwise, of any officer should be filled by the Board of Directors. In the event of a vacancy in any office other than that of President, such vacancy may be filled temporarily by appointment by the President until such time as the Board should fill the vacancy. Vacancies occurring in offices of officers appointed at the discretion of the board may or may not be filled as the board should determine.

Duties of President

The President should be the chief executive officer of the center and should, subject to the control of the Board of Directors, supervise and control the affairs of the center and the activities of the officers. He or she should perform all duties incident to his or her office and such other duties as may be required by law, by the Articles of Incorporation, or by these Bylaws, or which may be prescribed from time to time by the Board of Directors. Unless another person is specifically appointed as Chairperson of the Board of Directors, the President should preside at all meetings of the Board of Directors.

Duties of Vice President

In the absence of the President, or in the event of his or her inability or refusal to act, the Vice President should perform all the duties of the President, and when so acting should have all the powers of, and be subject to all the restrictions on, the President. The Vice President should have other powers and perform such other duties as may be prescribed by law, by the Articles of Incorporation, or by the Bylaws, or as may be prescribed by the Board of Directors.

Duties of Secretary

The Secretary should:

- Certify and keep at the principal office of the center the original, or a copy, of the Bylaws, as amended or otherwise altered to date.
- Keep at the principal office of the center or at such other place as the board may determine, a book of minutes of all meetings of the directors, and, if applicable, meetings of committees of directors and of members, recording therein the time and place of holding, whether regular or special, how called, how notice thereof was given, the names of those present or represented at the meeting, and the proceedings.
- Be custodian of the records and of the seal of the center and affix the seal, as authorized by law or the provisions of the Bylaws, to duly executed documents of the center.
- Keep at the principal office of the center a membership book containing the name and address of each and any members, and, in the case where any membership has been terminated, he or she should record such fact in the membership together with the date on which such membership ceased.
- Exhibit at all reasonable times to any director of the center, or to his or her agent or attorney, on request thereof, the Bylaws, the membership book, and the minutes of the proceedings of the directors of the center.In general, perform all duties incident to the office of Secretary and such other duties as may be required by law, by the Articles of Incorporation, or by the Bylaws, or which may be assigned to him or her from time to time by the Board of Directors

Duties of Treasurer

The Treasurer should:

- Have charge and custody of, and be responsible for, all funds and securities of the center, and deposit of all such funds in the name of the center in such banks, trust companies, or other depositories as should be selected by the Board of Directors.
- Receive, and give receipt for, monies due and payable to the center from any source whatsoever.
- Disburse, or cause to be disbursed, the funds of the center as may be directed by the Board of Directors, taking proper vouchers such disbursements.
- Keep and maintain adequate and correct accounts of the center's properties and business transactions, including accounts of its assets, liabilities, receipts, disbursements, gains and losses.
- Exhibit at all reasonable times the books of account and financial records to any director of the center, or to his or her agent or attorney, on request.
- Render to the President and directors, whenever requested, an account of any or all of his or her transactions as Treasurer and of the financial condition of the corporation.
- Prepare, or cause to be prepared, and certify, or cause to be certified, the financial statements to be included in any required reports.
- In general, perform all duties incident to the office of Treasurer and such other duties as may be required by law, by the Articles of Incorporation of the center, or by the Bylaws, or which may be assigned to him or her from time to time by the Board of Directors.

Compensation

The salaries of the officers, if any, should be fixed from time to time by resolution of the Board of Directors. In all cases, any salaries received by officers of the center should be reasonable and given in return for services actually rendered to or for the center.

COMMITTEES

Executive Committee

The Board of Directors may, by a majority vote of its members, designate an Executive Committee consisting of <u>three</u> board members and may delegate to such committee the powers and authority of the board in the management of the business and affairs of the center, to the extent permitted, and except as may otherwise be provided, by provisions of law.

By a majority vote of its members, the board may at any time revoke or modify any or all of the Executive Committee authority so delegated, increase or decrease but not below two (2) the number of the members of the Executive Committee, and fill vacancies on the Executive Committee from the members of the board. The Executive Committee should keep regular minutes of its proceedings, cause them to be filled with the center records, and report the same to the board from time to time as the board may require.

Other Committees

The center should have such other committees as may from time to time be designated by resolution of the Board of Directors. These committees may consist of persons who are not also members of the board and should act in an advisory capacity to the board.

Meetings and Action of Committees

Meetings and action of committees should be governed by, noticed, held and taken in accordance with the provisions of the Bylaws concerning meetings of the Board of Directors, with such changes in the context of such Bylaw provisions as are necessary to substitute the committee and its members for the Board of Directors and its members, except that the time for regular and special meetings of committees may be fixed by resolution of the Board of Directors or by the committee. The Board of Directors may also adopt rules and regulations pertaining to the conduct of meetings of committees to the extent that such rules and regulations are not inconsistent with the provisions of the Bylaws.

EXECUTION OF INSTRUMENTS, DEPOSITS AND FUNDS
Execution of Instruments

The Board of Directors, except as otherwise provided in the Bylaws, may by resolution authorize any officer or agent of the center to enter into any contract or execute and deliver any instrument in the name of and on behalf of the center, and such authority may be general or confined to specific instances. Unless so authorized, no officer, agent, or employee should have any power or authority to bind the center by any contract or engagement or to pledge its credit or to render it liable monetarily for any purpose or in any amount.

Checks and Notes

Except as otherwise specifically determined by resolution of the Board of Directors, or as otherwise required by law, checks, drafts, promissory notes, orders for the payment of money, and other evidence of indebtedness of the center should be signed by the Treasurer and countersigned by the President of the Center.

Deposits

All funds of the center should be deposited from time to time to the credit of the center in such banks, trust companies, or other depositories as the Board of Directors may select.

Gifts

The Board of Directors may accept on behalf of the center any contribution, gift, bequest, or devise for the nonprofit purposes of this center.

CORPORATE RECORDS, REPORTS AND SEAL
Maintenance of Corporate Records

The center should keep at its principal office:

a. Minutes of all meetings of directors, committees of the board and, if this center has members, of all meetings of members, indicating the time and place of holding such meetings, whether regular or special, how called, the notice given, and the names of those present and the proceedings thereof;

b. Adequate and correct books and records of account, including accounts of its properties and business transactions and accounts of its assets, liabilities, receipts, disbursements, gains and losses;

c. A record of its members, if any, indicating their names and addresses and, if applicable, the class of membership held by each member and the termination date of any membership;

d. A copy of the center's Articles of Incorporation and Bylaws as amended to date, which should be open to inspection by the members, if any, of the center at all reasonable times during office hours.

Corporate Seal

The Board of Directors may adopt, use, and at will alter, a corporate seal. Such seal should be kept at the principal office of the center. Failure to affix the seal to corporate instruments, however, should not affect the validity of any such instrument.

INSPECTION RIGHTS

Every director should have the absolute right at any reasonable time to inspect and copy all books, records and documents of every kind and to inspect the physical properties of the center and should have such other rights to inspect the books, records and properties of this center as may be required under the Articles of Incorporation, other provisions of the Bylaws, and provisions of law.

Member's Inspection Rights

If the center has any members, then each and every member should have the following inspection rights, for a purpose reasonably related to such person's interest as a member:

a.   To inspect and copy the record of all member's names, addresses and voting rights, at reasonable times, upon written demand on the Secretary of the center, which demand should state the purpose for which the inspection rights are requested

b.   To obtain from the Secretary of the center, upon written demand in, and payment of a reasonable charge to, the Secretary of the center, a list of the names, addresses and voting rights of those members entitled to vote for the election of directors as the most recent record date for which the list has been compiled or as of the date specified by the member subsequent to the date of demand. The demand should state the purpose for which the list is requested. The membership list should be made within a reasonable time after the demand.

c.   To inspect at any reasonable time the books, records, or minutes of proceedings of the members or of the board or committees of the board, upon written demand on the Secretary of the center by the member, for a purpose reasonably related to such person's interests as a member.

Members should have such other rights to inspect the books, records and properties of this center as may be required under the Articles of Incorporation, other provisions of the Bylaws, and provisions of law.

RIGHT TO COPY AND MAKE EXTRACTS
Develop special provisions for inspections and right to copy
Periodic Report

The board may have an annual or periodic report required under law to be prepared and delivered to an office of your location or to the members, if any, of this center, to be so prepared and delivered within the time limits set by law.

Limitations on Activities
Recommended where applicable in your location based on your tax status.

No substantial part of the activities of this center should be the carrying on of propaganda, or otherwise attempting to influence legislation [except as otherwise provided by Section 501 (of the Internal Revenue Code], and this center should not participate in, or intervene in (including the publishing or distribution of statements), any political campaign on behalf of, or in opposition to, any candidate for public office.

Notwithstanding any other provisions of the Bylaws, this center should not carry on any activities not permitted to be carried on (a) by a center exempt from federal income tax under Section 501(c)(3) of the Internal Revenue Code, or (b) by a corporation, contributions to which are deductible under Section 170(c)(2) of the Internal Revenue Code.

Prohibition Against Private Inurement
Recommended where applicable in your location based on your tax status.

No part of the net earnings of this center should inure to the benefit of, or be distributable to, its members, directors or trustees, officers, or other private persons, except that the center should be authorized and empowered to pay reasonable compensation for services rendered and to make payments and distributions in furtherance of the purposes of this center.

Distribution of Assets

Recommended where applicable in your location based on your tax status.

Upon the dissolution of this center, its assets remaining after payment, or provision for payment, of all debts and liabilities of this center should be distributed for one or more exempt purposes within the meaning of Section 510(c)(3) of the Internal Revenue Code or should be distributed to the federal government, or to a state or local government, for a public purpose. Such distribution should be made in accordance with all applicable provisions of the laws of this state.

Private Foundation Requirements and Restrictions

Recommended where applicable in your location based on your tax status.

In any taxable year in which this center is a private foundation as described in Section 509(a) of the Internal Revenue Code, the center 1) should distribute its income for said period at such time and manner as not to subject it to tax under Section 4942 of the Internal Revenue Code; 2) should not engage in any act of self-dealing as defined in Section 4941(d) of the Internal Revenue Code; 3)should not retain any excess business holdings as defined in Section 4943(c) of the Internal Revenue Code; 4) should not make any investments in such as to subject the center to tax under Section 4944 of the Internal Revenue Code; and 5) should not make any taxable expenditures as defined in Section 4945(d) of the Internal Revenue Code.

AMENDMENT OF BYLAWS
Amendment

Subject to the power of the members, if any, of this center to adopt, amend or repeal the Bylaws of this center and except as may otherwise be specified under provisions of law, the Bylaws, or any of them, may be altered, amended, or repealed and new Bylaws adopted by approval of the Board of Directors.

CONSTRUCTION AND TERMS

If there is any conflict between the provisions of the Bylaws and the Articles of Incorporation of this center, the provisions of the Articles of Incorporation should govern.

Should any of the provisions or portions of the Bylaws be held unenforceable or invalid for any reason, the remaining provisions and portions of the Bylaws should be unaffected by such holding.

All references in the Bylaws to the Articles of Incorporation should be to the Articles of Incorporation, Articles of Organization, Certificate of Incorporation, Organizational Charter, Corporate Charter, or other founding document of this center filed with an office of your location and used to establish the legal existence of this center.

SUMMARY

Securing nurturing environments and effective parenting practices are a few of the family processes associated with family education centers and normative child development (Cicchetti et al., 1995; Cowan & Cowan, 2002). Master's level counseling students can greatly benefit from such a rich supportive experience received from their involvement with a Family Education Center. For example, in the past decade, 46 states have granted a master's degree level family therapy license recognized by most third-party payers. Family-Centered treatment programs have increased the delivery of community based services for public mental health and substance abuse programs (Chavez & Kumpfer, 1998; Nelson, 1997). Family education centers have been recognized as best practice models in reports by the National Institutes of Drug Abuse and Mental Health, the Office of Juvenile Justice, the Center for Substance Abuse Treatment, the U.S. Surgeon General and many private organizations (Child Trends, 2002; Mihalic et al., 2001;

National Advisory Mental Health Workgroup on Child and Adolescent Mental Health Intervention Development and Deployment, 2001; U.S. Department of Health and Human Services, 1999). The rewards and benefits are numerous, both professionally and financially. Master's level students should be aware of the positive benefits of networking with universities, colleges, government agencies, private treatment programs, church groups, and community partners, where they are working with a center or establishing a family education center.

REFERENCES

Chavez, N. & Kumpfer, K. L (1998). Family involvement is key to preventing child adolescent substance abuse. Available at: http://alt.samhsa.gov/news/newreleases/980603p.html.

Child Trends (2002). Building a better teenager: A summary of what works in adolescent development. Online reported November 25. Available at: http://www.childtrends.org/files/K7Brief.pdf.

Cicchetti, D., Toth, S.L., & Lynch, M. (1995). Bowlby's dream come full circle: The application of attachment theory to risk and psychopathology. *Advance Clinical Child Psychology* 17: 1–75.

Cowan, P.A., & Cowan, C.P. (2002). Interventions as tests of family systems theories: Marital and family relationships in children's development and psychopathology. *Dev Psychopathology* 14:731–759.

Freeman, J.B., Garcia, A.M., Fucci, C., Karitani, M., Miller, L., Leonard, H.L. (2003). Family-based treatment of early-onset obsessive-compulsive disorder. *J Child Adolescent Psychopharmacology* 13:S71–S80.

McDonough, J. (2003). Approaches to Adlerian family education research. University of Minnesota.

Mihalic, S., Irwin, K., Elliott, D., Fagan, A., & Hansen, D. (2001). *Blueprints for violence prevention.* Boulder, CO: Center for the study of violence prevention.

National Advisory Mental Health Workgroup on Child and Adolescent Mental Health Intervention Development and Deployment (2001). *Blueprint for change: Research on Child and adolescent mental health.* Washington, D.C.: National Institute of Mental Health.

Nelson, K.E. (1997). Family preservation. What is it? *Child Youth Services Rev* 19:101–118.

Rutter, M. (2002). The interplay of nature, nurture, and developmental influences: The challenge ahead for mental health. *Arch Gen Psychiatry* 59:996–1000.

U.S. Department of Health and Human Services (1999). *Mental health: A report of the surgeon general.* Rockville, Maryland: U.S. Department of Health and Human Services, Substance Abuse and Mental Health Administration, Center for Mental Health Services, National Institutes of Health, National Institute of Mental Health.

Weisz, J.B., Doneberg, G.B., Han S.S., Kauneckis, D. (1995). Child and adolescent psychotherapy outcome in experiments verse clinic: Why the disparity. *J Abnormal Child Psychology* 23:83–106.

Section Three

*Counseling Competencies and
Professional Development*

The Importance of Becoming a Multicultural Counselor in all Settings

9

By Jake Johnson, Ph.D.

In becoming an effective competent counselor across-culture, it is crucial to examine and discuss the core fundamental attributes of professional helpers. The self-understanding of professional counselors' baseline personality traits and characteristics that are needed in pursuing a career in the counseling field is primary. There are several components that are needed and suggested for trainees in counseling programs that include awareness, knowledge, skill development and experiential interaction (Ibrahim, 1991; Loesch, 1988; and Pederson, 1994). Recognizing that professional counselors are all products of their environments and the sum total of their life experiences i.e. psychosocial development, familial experiences, religious teachings and experiences, formal and informal education and the like, reinforces the constant need for self-awareness. In addition to the basic skills and awareness that professional counselors should possess, it is also crucial that an acute comprehension of personal biases, cognitions, views and perspectives of people across-culture are maintained (Arredondo, Toporek, Brown, Jones, Locke, Sanchez, and Stadler, (1996); Vontress, 2008, 2005, 2003).

This chapter will focus on counseling from a multicultural perspective. It will provide students with information on counseling competencies needed in preparation for a professional counseling career in counseling clients across-cultures from diverse backgrounds. The chapter will also challenge students to examine their biases and stereotypical beliefs of culturally different clients and to embrace other cultures with knowledge, dignity and respect. From the board room to the classroom, this chapter will provide counselors with information needed to address culturally diverse populations in all settings and to seek the type of training required in becoming a competent multicultural counselor.

SELF-UNDERSTANDING

Emerging professional counselors must not take the need to possess an in-depth self-understanding for granted. Although self-understanding is a dynamic process, it is one that must be highly developed by the neophyte counselor as well as the experienced professional counselor. Inherent in this process, is an awareness of counselors' biases—subjective cognitions that are akin to their belief system, perspectives and views of others across-cultures (Combs, 1986; Sue, 1992; Lee, 1989; Lee, C. C., & Richardson, B. L. 1991). In an attempt in remaining aware of the mentally recorded experiential world of the budding professional counselor, it becomes plausible to surface their unconscious motivators. That is, counselors work to meet and greet their own thoughts about the world and all that exist in it. Recognizing the mental processing of subjective images and information that directly connect to the creation and existence of a perceived culturally different defined person, becomes a formable cognizant task for counselors seeking greater levels of effectiveness as practitioners (Ramirez, 1999; Sue, 1992;Vontress, 2003). The critical developmental mark for aspiring professional counselors is the conscious ability to remain ever present of their own subjective beliefs. The ability and the application to be able to separate counselors' world—assumptions and beliefs, from that of their clients' are immeasurable.

TRAINING AND EDUCATION

The training and formal education of perspective professional counselors are priceless. As a result, it becomes imperative that all counselor training/counselor education programs establish and implement a holistic approach to pedagogy, curriculum development and its application. The American Counseling Association (ACA) Code of Ethics (2005) supports this position. However, it is egregious and unconscionable that far too many counselor education programs have opposing convert philosophical differences with establishing comprehensive multicultural/cross-cultural components intricately throughout their counseling programs (Pederson, 1988). Simply stated, many do not believe that the need does exist for the teaching of multicultural counseling and training for multicultural counselors in our wonderful diverse and multicultural world. In maintaining a direct relationship between training and practice, it is consistently necessary to connect counselor education training with the population that it is and will be serving. The world is a very cultural place and such the need exists to understudy people across-cultures—their traditions, customs, practices, languages, religion, spiritual beliefs, family, community, physical/biological self and environmental worlds, interpersonal world, their private or psychological world, political ideology, regional and national views, experiences with racism, oppression, social injustice and the like (Lee, 1991; Arredondo et al., 1996; Vontress, Johnson & Epp, 1999).

Journeying toward the actualization of becoming an effective professional counselor, neophyte counselors are called to be extremely cautious about the one fits all clients theoretical orientation. Vontress (1979, 1983, 2003) in his work and research on cross-cultural and existential counseling warms counselors about the "cookbook" approach to counseling the culturally different client. Corey (2008) strongly suggests that group counselors avoid encapsulating their clients. According to Sue (1992), there must be recognition among programs providing training that there is not a single theory or approach of helping that will be fitting for all clients and their challenges. Counselors must continue to put their clients first in the counseling process. Clients' diagnosis and assessment are not relegated to any one particular theoretical counseling approach. Positioning themselves to become active listeners in the counseling relationship, might assist counselors in becoming effective practitioners. By providing clients the opportunity to share their cultural experiences and related meanings, establishes the groundwork for the attainment of a more accurate assessment. After all, one of the major functions of a professional counselor is to understand the self-perceptive world of the client. In his research on identifying the characteristics of an effective counselor/helper, Combs (1986) studies suggest that one of the five characteristics of an effective helper is the "beliefs about the value of focusing on the client's personal world." His work provides evidence of the importance of counselors focusing on the internal world or worldview perspective of clients. His work prior that of Arredondo et al. (1996) gives excellent support to their position on "counselor awareness of client's worldview."

Given the history of any particular cultural group, it is paramount that professional counselors educate themselves on the historical events of the various cultural groups. However, caution about the generalizing effect of cultural history must be omnipresent in the consciousness of counseling professionals. In essence, it is imperative that professional counselors do not impose their perceptions and understanding about clients' cultural history on them. This approach becomes a critical one in adhering to the comprehension of individuals' self-perceptions about the impact of and their identification with their cultural historical experiences. Simply stated, this procedure provides the direct linkage needed by counselors in maintaining an understanding of the worldview of clients. Furthermore, by addressing the cognitions of clients, counselors are more able to recognize how clients are identifying with the history of their culture (Vontress, Johnson, & Epp, 1999).

Enough cannot be said about the value of professional development and research for professional counselors. Beyond the traditional modes of professional development through conferences, workshops, seminars and symposiums, there is an ongoing need for professional counselors to dedicate time with those from different cultures in their environments i.e. homes, places worship, cultural activities and events, foreign countries, ethnic and cultural restaurants, educational facilities and the like to develop a greater understanding how clients' experiences eventuate.

COLLECTIVISTIC VERSUS INDIVIDUALISTIC

There is need for professional counselors to develop their awareness about collectivistic and individualistic elements of cultural groups (Triandis, 1994). The assessment of individuals across-culture requires a level of awareness and understanding of what extent clients are functioning on a collectivistic perspective—individuals' perspectives/perceptions about life and behavior that are highly connected to the good of the family, friends, neighbors, the neighborhood, community, the nation and the like. Collectivistic behavior is expressed through individuals maintaining "their personal goals" as being secondary to those of their respective group (Ady, 1998). Conversely, individuals who are individualistic tend to be more perceptually focused on functions and behaviors that are not family, community, neighborhood and group oriented and are more likely to focus on personal wants, needs and desires (Hofstede, 1980). For example, clients who identify highly with their family, friends and community might desire to involve other family members in the counseling process. This perception might be closely associated with collectivistic clients' having the need of belonging and strongly perceiving their functioning in the world as closely being associated with and connected to others or their identified cultural group (Triandis, Brislin, & Hui, 1991). The converse is believed to be representing those who are individualistic. Demonstrating characteristics that are intimately associated with an effective counselor can be measured by professional counselors' ability to work within the internal framework or perceptual field of clients. Counselors must be mindful that clients from collectivistic backgrounds, through assimilation experiences, might not highly identify with this perspective. The existence of this variation in the cultural identification process again supports professional counselors' need to sustain a direct alignment with clients' personal/psychological world (Vontress, 1979, 1983).

ASSESSMENT OF CLIENTS ACROSS-CULTURE

Assessing clients across-culture or from a multicultural perspective in the counseling relationship is a multifaceted and intricate process.

Again, professional counselors are cautioned to be acutely aware of their beliefs, attitudes, knowledge, and skills (Combs 1986; Arredondo et al., 1996). Emphasis is placed on the methodology, tools/instruments and the appropriateness of questions asked in the multicultural counseling relationship. Instruments that do not reflect or represent the cultural experiences of clients must not be used in the assessment process. Counselor must be skilled in the use of assessment instruments. Assessing clients across-culture requires that professional counselors are aware of or become aware of their stereotypical beliefs of and any subsequent behaviors toward culturally different clients. Stereotyping by professional counselors of clients is seen as generalizing the behaviors of clients to others in their respective cultural group. In assessing clients' major life concerns, professional counselors continue to work within the internal framework of them. Developing an accurate assessment requires that counselors continue to work within the perceptual sphere of the clients by avoiding the traditional labeling process or DMS-IVing—using the Diagnostic and Statistical Manual of Mental Disorders, Fourth Edition-Revised (DSM-IV-TR) of culturally different clients without any relevant case information (American Psychiatric Association, 1994; Vontress, Johnson & Epp, 1999). From a multicultural prospective, assessment of clients should be executed by developing a holistic view of their experiences and the meaning(s) that has been placed on them. Professional counselors must not impose their values and attitudes about the assessment process onto clients. They must remain cognizant of their personal views and differences and of those that exist in the personal psychological world of clients (Combs, 1986; Arredondo et al., 1996; Vontress, Johnson, & Epp, 1999).

Empathy is one of the most powerful counseling skills that professional counselors can employ in the counseling relationship in general and particularly in the assessment of individuals across-cultures (Rogers, 1961). Professional counselors must demonstrate their ability to enter into the world of their clients. The process of empathizing with clients is characterized by counselors' precise understanding of clients' experiential and perceptual worlds. In this assessment process, counselors can display a sense of awareness of the clients' personal understanding by communicating their comprehension of the clients' shared experiences. The elements of this empathic counseling experience are further characterized by counselors' accurate interpretation skills. At this juncture, counselors are able to provide relevant meaning to what the clients' have stated. It is required that counselors continue to connect themselves to personal visions of their clients. Moreover, the assessment of the clients' worldview and human condition rest upon the counselors' ability in remaining value neutral—not imposing any personal values and subjective feelings and cognitions on clients. Although the individual and cultural characteristics are important in the assessment and intervention of culturally different and diverse clients, it is as equally necessary, if not greater, to assess clients' level of identification with their culture (Vontress, Johnson, & Epp, 1999).

The move to use specific techniques in the multicultural counseling relationship may have little utility (Vontress, 1979). As professional counselors travel deeper into the world of cross-cultural counseling, it appears that the assessment and intervention strategies are giving way to appropriate approaches, understanding of the worldview of clients, awareness of counselors' cultural valves and biases, and culturally appropriate intervention strategies, and the beliefs and attitudes, knowledge, and skills that are attached to them (Ibrahim, 1991; Loesch, 1988; & Pederson, 1994; Arredondo et al., 1996). Underscoring the four worlds of clients'—biological/physical, interpersonal, private/psychological and spiritual worlds capture the essence of human existence. Without imposing counselors' values and attitudes on clients, full assessment and intervention strategies might be appropriately developed, as they are directly filtered through the visions and images of clients' private or personal world (Vontress, 1979, 1983; Vontress, Johnson, & Epp, 1999). Consequently, the elements of all that are multicultural in the world of the clients are shared expressively, to the extent that their identification with their culture permits them, by them. Helping clients to develop a deeper self-understanding and awareness, remains the focal point of the multicultural counseling relationship. Succinctly, there appears to be no room for monolithic approaches in assisting professional counselors in becoming effective multicultural practitioners.

Professional counselors must position themselves to be aware of the different levels of sharing in the cross-cultural counseling relationship (Sue, 1991, 1992; Vontress, Johnson, & Epp, 1999). Many clients across-culture or culturally different clients may not be willing to self-disclose because of their identification with their interest group i.e. family and cultural group. The focus of these clients is placed on the interest of their group and not themselves. Many clients might feel that it is impolite to draw attention to themselves and not their immediate group members. Counselors must also develop a broad understanding of the concept of resistance. Clients might be in conflict with their family values and beliefs prohibiting them from openly sharing information in a counseling relationship. Filial piety might be a major stressor and concern for some Chinese Americans in counseling relationships. Their allegiance to their parents might not be recognized by the professional counselor and could be a prohibiting force to the sharing of information within the counseling relationship (Sue, 1991). Sue (1991) suggests that Chinese Americans adherence to filial piety provides "little room for self-determination." Given the variations in cultural experiences across-cultures, it is critical that professional counselors maintain a sense of awareness about their understanding of resistance and pursue inquiry in an attempt to developing some insight of it. In a very cautious and culturally sensitive approach, counselors must seek to discover the why behind the perceived resistant behavior of their clients. Implications here might suggest that the conceptualization of the concept of "resistance" be redefined and re-conceptualized in the light of varying cultural contexts of behaviors and intercultural and personal worldviews that might exist.

Countertransference in the counseling relationship can become a major prohibiting force in the assessment and intervention process of multicultural clients. Corey and Corey (1988) suggest that the presence of countertransference in the counseling relationship might "interfere" with counselors' "objectivity." The mere understanding of this psycho-analytic concept places the existence of unconscious psychological material of the counseling professional into the multicultural counseling experience with clients. However, recognizing its presence in the cross-cultural counseling relationship substantiates the ongoing need for counselors remaining cognizant of their subjective but yet unconscious biases, beliefs, perceptions and cognitions of the culturally different client. Although counselors might not be free of countertransference, it is vital that they become aware of how it can impact the counseling relationship (Corey & Corey, 1993, 1998). Competent and caring counseling professionals seek to explore and examine their personal understandings of persons across-culture and learn to delineate and become more conscious of their subjective cognitions, visions, images, and beliefs.

Recapitulating, the need remains constant for the ongoing training of professional counselors helping clients' across-culture. Self-understanding holds the key to the awareness of counselors' biases, beliefs, attitudes and knowledge of self and of others. Being able to separate their subjective world from that of their clients becomes a critical task for aspiring competent professional counselors. By working to maintain an understanding of the worldview of clients, without imposing their values and attitudes on them, positions emerging counseling professionals in becoming competent helpers. The value of comprehensive counselor education and training programs are invaluable. Multicultural /cross-cultural counseling and education components must be intricate parts of the curriculum. Counselors are cautioned about the practice of a monolithic theoretical approach to counseling clients across-culture. Emphasizing the professional counselors' ability in understanding the clients' personal or private world over the use of traditional counseling theories and techniques, might more effectively assist clients in regaining control of their lives. In developing their understanding of clients' personal worlds, counselors must consider the impact of clients' collectivistic and individualistic backgrounds and experiences, and to the extent how they might influence clients' functioning and sharing of information in the counseling relationship. Assessment of clients in the multicultural counseling relationship must not be placed highly on the use of psychometric instruments and other traditional testing procedures. Rather, counselors must be skilled at using empathy in developing an understanding of the clients' worldview.

Central to the effectiveness of multicultural counselors is their ability and skill in remaining in the world of clients. Being attached to the personal world of clients can serve as an effective tool in assisting across-culture clients in reestablishing control of their lives.

REFERENCES

Ady, J.C. (1998). Negotiating across cultural boundaries: Implications of individualism-collectivism and cases and application. In T.M. Sigelis (Ed.), *Teaching about culture, ethnicity, and diversity* (pp. 111–120). Thousand Oaks, CA: Sage.

American Counseling Association (2005). *The ACA code of ethics*. Alexandria, VA: Author.

American Psychiatric Association. (1994). *Diagnostic and statistical manual of mental disorders*, (4th ed.). Washington, DC: Author.

Arredondo, P., Toporek, M. S., Brown, S., Jones, J., Locke, D.C., Sanchez, J. & Stadler, H. (1996). *Operationalization of the multicultural counseling competencies. Journal of Multicultural Counseling and Development*, 24 (1), 42–78.

Combs, A. W. (1986). What makes a good helper? A person-centered approach. *Person Centered Review*, 191, 51–61.

Corey, G. (2008). *Theory and practice of group counseling* (7th ed.). Pacific Grove, CA: Brooks/Cole.

Corey, M. S., Corey, G. (1993). *Becoming a helper* (2nd ed.). Belmont, CA: Brooks/Cole.

Corey, M. S., Corey, G. (1993). *Becoming a helper* (3rd ed.). Belmont, CA: Brooks/Cole.

Hofestede, G. (1980). *Culture's consequences: International differences in work-related values*. Beverly Hills, CA: Sage.

Ibrahim, F. A. (1991). Contribution of cultural worldview to generic counseling and development. *Journal of Counseling and Development*, 70(1), 13–19.

Ivey, A. E. (1992). Caring and commitment: are you up to the challenge of multicultural counseling and therapy? *Guidepost*, 34(9), 16.

Lee, C. C. (1989). Multicultural counseling: New directions for counseling professionals. *Virginia Counselors Journal*, 17, 3–8.

Lee, C. C. (1991). Cultural dynamics their importance in multicultural counseling. In Lee, C. C., & Richardson, B. L (Eds.), *Multicultural issues in counseling: New approaches to diversity* (pp. 3–8). Alexandra, VA: American Association for Counseling and Development.

Lee, C. C., & Richardson, B. L. (1991). Promise and pitfalls of multicultural counseling. In Lee, C. C., & Richardson, B. L (Eds.), *Multicultural issues in counseling: New approaches to diversity* (pp. 3–8). Alexandra, VA: American Association for Counseling and Development.

Loesch, L. C. (1988). Preparation for helping professionals working with diverse populations. In N. A. Vacc, J. Wittmer, & S. B. DeVaney (Eds.), *Experiencing and counseling diverse populations* (2nd ed.) (pp. 317–340). Muncie, IN: Accelerated Development.

Pederson, P. (1988). *A handbook for developing multicultural awareness*. Alexandria, VA: American Association for Counseling and Development.

Pederson, P. (1994). *A handbook for developing multicultural awareness* (2nd ed.) Alexandria, VA: American Counseling Association.

Ramirez, M. (1999). *Multicultural psychotherapy: An approach to individual and cultural differences* (2nd ed.). Needham Heights, MA: Allyn and Bacon.

Rogers, C. (1961). *On becoming a person*. Boston: Houghton Mifflin

Sue, D. W. (1991). Counseling strategies for Chinese Americans. In C. C. Lee, B. L. Richardson (Eds.), *Multicultural issues in counseling: New approaches to Diversity* (pp. 70–90). Alexandra, VA: American Association for Counseling and Development.

Sue, D. W. (1992). The challenge of multiculturalism: The road less traveled. *American Counselor*, 1(1), 6–14.

Triandis, H. C. (1990). Cross-cultural studies on individualism and collectivism. In R. A. Diehstbier & J. J. Berman (Eds.), *Nebraska symposium on 1989* (pp. 31–132). Lincoln: University of Nebraska Press.

Triandis, H. C., Brislin, R., & Hui, C. (1991). Cross-cultural training across the individualism and collectivism divide. In L. Samovar & R. Porter (Eds.), *Intercultural communication: A reader* (pp. 370–382). Belmont, CA: Wadsworth.

Vontress, C. E. (1979). Cross-cultural counseling: An Existential approach. *The Personnel and Guidance Journal*, 58, 117–122.

Vontress, C. E. (1983). An existential approach to cross-cultural counseling. *Counseling and Values*, 28, 2–12.

Vontress, C. E. (2003). On becoming an existential cross-cultural counselor. In F. D. Harper & J. McFadden (Eds.), *Culture and counseling* (pp. 20–30). Boston: Allyn and Bacon.

Vontress, C. E. (2005). On becoming an existential school counselor. *School Counselor*, 42(6), 8–12.

Vontress, C. E. (2008). Existential therapy. In J, Frew, & M. D. Spiegler (Eds.), *Contemporary psychotherapies for a diverse world* (pp. 141–176). Boston: Houghton Mifflin/Lahaska Press.

Vontress, C. E., Johnson, J. A., & Epp, L. R. (1999). *Cross-cultural counseling: A case book*. Alexandria, VA: American Counseling Association.

Legal and Ethical Issues in Therapy

10

By Henry Raymond, Ph.D.

The profession of counseling and psychotherapy demands the complete and committed attention of the practitioner for the maintenance of an effective practice. Beyond the learning of theories of counseling, the practitioner in training should seriously challenge himself/herself in terms of his or her commitment to the field of counseling from the perspective of "why" and "how" does this field match his/her "passion" for life. Only after this assessment has been made and one has moved beyond the possible hidden personal constructs of entering the field for the purpose of self-healing, self-improvement and finding solutions to unresolved childhood issues can serious attention be given and focused upon the magnitude of understanding the legal and ethical ramifications pertinent to the mental health field. This field is about helping and facilitating clients in finding means and processes to solve their own problems and concerns independently.

From the beginning the practitioner should equip himself or herself with a thorough understanding of the ethical standards governing the mental health field so as to operate at all times in an ethical manner. Ethics Codes are produced and distributed by each professional association; therefore, the practitioner is expected to adhere to the ethical codes of his/her professional association. A common definition of ethics is that of what is "good" or "right." Professional ethics within the mental health field implies good or acceptable practices. Morality (morals) often refers to acts or behavior with some reference to cultural, regional or social stance or a religious base or established and recognized codes of behavior.

MAKING ETHICAL DECISIONS

As professionals in the field of counseling psychology, mental health practitioners are expected to become active members of the chosen associations. These organizations have defined "professional" and "legally-mandated" ethic codes as well an "inspirational" codes of ethics that are promoted for its members to adhere to in their practices (Corey, et al, 2007). Beyond the "professional" ethics are the "legally" mandated legal requirements which mean that certain laws have been passed and referenced in state's licensure statutes that must be adhered to in their practices. The violations of such statutes could result in licensure revocation or suspension; therefore, the professional and legally mandated ethics must be upheld and adhered to at all time.

In cases or situations where there is little or no guidance to guide the practitioner in making an "ethical decision" in concert with his or her client, the practitioner will need to refer to a proven process for reaching an ethical decision. It is reasonable to assume that all solutions to all given dilemmas will not or cannot be found in text materials; therefore, the practitioner might consider the suggested models devised by Welfel (2005), Cottone, (2001), Hill, Glaser, and Harden (1995) and others for making ethical decisions. Hill, Glaser, and Harden (1995) suggest seven steps which have been cited by Corey, et al, (2007 p. 20) as a model for reaching an ethical decision where little or guidance in available:

- Recognize a problem
- Defining the problem—network with your therapeutic team
- Developing solutions with client
- Choosing a solution
- Reviewing the process with the client and assessing results, re-choosing
- Implementing and evaluating the process with your client\
- Continuing reflection

BRIEFING GUIDE/INFORMED CONSENT

During the early stages of developing an effective counseling profession, the wise practitioner utilizes the prepared informed consent statement or briefing guide to complete the theoretical frame work for his services.

The development of a well-developed informed consent statement or form is viewed as essential for adherence to and upholding the ethical and legal standards in the field of psychotherapy. The informed consent statement or form will be presented to the client during the initial session and explained in sufficient details continuously until the client become thoroughly educated on all facets of the document. Most authors support the notion of developing an informed consent statement prior to the commencement of therapeutic services where the therapeutic stance of the practitioner is delineated in detail to the client (Corey et al., 2007, Gill, 1982; Gross, 1977; Swanson, 1979; Winborn, 1977). This document should include, least in part, key aspects of the client's Bill of Rights, which delineates the rights of each client and should be known by clients that these are their rights which are fully supported by the Ethics Codes of ACE (2005, A.2.b), APA (2002, 10.01), and other mental health associations such as The American Mental Health Counselors Association (2000, Principle I.J.) The intent of the Bill of Rights of Clients is to secure clients full participation in the process and to ensure that they are educated on the procedures and processes involved in services provided.

According to New Direction Counseling (http://www.newdirectionscounseling.com/billright.html), the Client Bill of Rights may be summarized in many formats, nevertheless, the essential issues are:

- Receive services in a respectful way that's helpful
- Receive specific services or end such services without duress or harassment
- Receive such services in a safe environment free of sexual, physical and emotional abuse

- Encourage clients to submit reports of unethical or illegal behaviors by practitioner
- Encourage clients to ask questions about their services and expectations
- Receive complete information concerning practitioners professional capabilities, including licensing, education, training, experience, membership in professional associations and specialties.
- May refuse or accept recordings in sessions
- May refuse to answer various types of question or to give certain type of information
- To be educated on the Limits of Confidentiality and the situations in which the practitioner is legally required to disclose information to others including the authorities
- Be told if there are colleagues, supervisors, consultants, students, or others whom the practitioner will be discussing the clients case, including HMOs.
- Have full access to your files and reports
- May request the transmission of your file to another professional or agency
- May receive a second opinion at any time
- Request progress evaluations from your practitioner at any time

A well designed and informative briefing guide or informed consent document can serve as a meaningful way to educate the client about the services provided. It should also serve the practitioner well in defending against malpractice claims. When constructed with due care, the briefing guide/informed consent should include the practitioner's educational background, pertinent background in the field such as qualifications in specific specialties, theoretical counseling stance and practices, expectations during the counseling process, an overview of the limits of confidentiality, payment process and emergency procedures. The briefing guide should serve as a "roadmap" for the counseling process so that there will be no surprises in the process and what client can be easily educated on the basic elements of the entire process.

The legal and ethical aspects of the informed consent document must be written clearly in understandable language in preparation for clients, the practitioner entertains and upholds the basic tenet of "ethical standards in counseling and therapy." The legal aspect of the informed consent may be summarized in the following three categories: capacity, comprehension of data, and voluntariness (Anderson, 1996; Corey et al, 2007). The practitioner must ensure that clients have the capacity to make and rational decisions, to comprehend information that is given to them in a meaningful way and that the client is qualified and able to give an informed consent. The legal aspects of counseling or therapy should involve an educational process by which the practitioner can attest to the understanding of the information by the client. These attributes are met through interviews and intake procedures prior to the beginning of the formal process of therapy.

CONFIDENTIALITY, PRIVILEGED COMMUNICATION AND PRIVACY

The ethic codes of mental health organizations address the basic concepts of standards associated with confidentiality, privileged communication and privacy. The following definitions should illustrate the significant differences between each of these concepts:

- Confidentiality: Is an ethical entity and is supported by the ethic codes of various mental health organizations.
- Privileged communication: Privileged communication is a legal entity and was a judgment that grew out of the Jeffee v. Redmond case, which stated that privileged communication was required for effective psychotherapy to occur between a therapist and his/her client.

Privacy

Privacy is a legal entity and is protected by the Constitution of the United States of American, which intimates that individuals have the right to decide to whom, where and when personal information about themselves may be divulged.

Through an educational process by the practitioner on the informed consent form (or briefing guide), the practitioner ensures that the client understands the limitations of confidentiality, and the practitioner's responsibilities when confidentiality must be broken. Due to current laws all child abuse cases (physical abuse, sexual abuse, neglect cases, and mal-emotional treatment of children), regardless when the offense occurred, must be reported and abuse of the elderly must also be reported, as well as destruction of property, in mandated court cases and in cases involving malpractice suits. In connection with these issues, the storage of progress notes should be explained so the client can readily understand the efforts put in place to protect and to secure the client's documents and to ensure that the confidentiality of such documents will not be compromised.

Practitioner secure and maintain filing cabinets to house such documents for at least seven years whereby the confidentiality of such materials will not be exposed to non-authorized persons. Safeguarding and securing counseling progress notes, tests, and other materials offer one of the best defense against a malpractice suites. It is crucial that only authorized persons have access to client files. Some of the material may be very sensitive and very damaging to extended family members or to public figures if exposed. Once progress notes have been filed, they are never to altered or changed.

The management of confidential data and information pertaining to client's health requires a thorough understanding and appreciation of the limits of confidentiality. A brief summation of the limits of confidentiality, which is commonly depicted in various professional codes and psychological digests are:

a.   Cases of suspected child abuse;
b.   Cases of suspected elderly abuse;

c.   Cases involved with the destruction of property;

d.   Cases where individuals has stated an intention (threats) of causing harm to individuals, groups of individuals or to society as a whole;

e.   Cases involving counseling of minor children and the parent or legal guardian requests case information;

f.   Cases studies involving colleagues with whom the practitioner/ therapist networks or an intern supervisee in such a way that the identifying data has been extracted from the case notes.

Having cited reference to the limits of confidentiality in the informed consent form or briefing guide now fosters a seamless detailed explanation of this concept. It is essential that the client is educated on the limits of confidentiality because it is the linchpin which is under girding the entire therapeutic process and its limitations within the professional ethical and legal boundaries of the field. Clients should be informed that practitioner can share the client's information with others only if the client gives the practitioner written permission to do so.

DANGEROUSNESS AND APPROPRIATE DIAGNOSES

Given the ever increasing violence reported in elementary, middle, high schools, and young adults (age 18–34) across America, (Bureau of Justice, 2005) there is a need for institutions preparing candidates to become effective practitioners and therapy, to include in their training programs instruction on how to identify and treat dangerous clients. In such training of candidates to practice in the mental health field, the following topics should be thoroughly discussed Ohlschlager (2008) and Moline(1997):

- Record of client's prior violent behaviors
- Diagnosis of current status
- Keep accurate records of treatment
- Encourage client to maintain contact with certain people

- Availability or access to lethal weapons
- Enlist the assistance of family members and friends
- Use informed consent approach in dealing with colleagues, psychiatrists, or others
- When warning third parties provide only the essential information necessary
- History of substance abuse
- History of family support system
- Assessment of stress management skills
- Assessment of meaning of life
- Assessment of values and spirituality
- Increase the frequency of therapeutic sessions

Ohlschlager (ecounseling.com) (2008) has also provided suggestions for clinical assessment of dangerous clients:

- the assessment process should include the following items current risk, past behavior, family history of violence, drug use/ abuse, psychological/personality disorders, and relevant demographic and situational factors; and
- review the assessment evidence to ascertain there are reasonable and verifiable evidence of dangerousness as to:
- define the communicated threat of violence or intent to harm
- ascertain that that is serious, doable, and imminent
- the threat is directed against an identified or reasonably identifiable victim(s).

To support this effort he suggested that the therapist should make careful notations on the client's prior history of threats and violent behaviors; also, ensure that a careful study is conducted of his/her family history involving violent behaviors. Ohlschlager (2008) stated that "the best predictor of future violence is a history or pattern of past violence" (p. 1). A thorough interview of all applicable persons should be made and care notes should be filed and analyzed. During case consultation or networking sessions, practitioners should consult with their professional treatment team—the psychiatrist, attorney, and colleagues ensure that all appropriate steps are taken to fully understand the client's likely behavior including the direction and its likely severity.

The exploration of procedures and strategies for dealing with dangerous clients should lead to an exhaustive review of clients with suicidal tendencies or suicidal ideation constructs. Due to the broad escalation of reported suicide ideation from the middle school through college; then into the adulthood serious consideration and preparation should be taken to understand and treat this growing phenomena (Ohlschlager, 2008). As a minimum, new practitioners might create a "suicidal checklist" to be used in the prevention of a suicide, which is prominently displayed for rapid access for review and action. Since the destruction of one's life constitutes ground for breaking confidentiality, practitioners have the responsibility of warning family members or spouses. An assessment of the clients capability to carry out the threat of suicide by carefully monitoring and documenting the activities of the client as to: (www.fda.gov).

- disposing personal items
- dramatic changes in habits
- discussing the lack of interest in the meaning of life
- indicating perhaps this is the last time "we" might be able to see each other
- loss of interest in favorite sports, activities, rituals, or food
- loss of interest in intimacy and sexual activities
- discussion of not needing things or preparations for the future
- assess the client for psychological issues such as depression, schizophrenia, drug abuse and conduct disorders
- seeking revenge, anger and rage
- committing risky behaviors or recklessness

Clients who threaten suicidal intentions or have suicidal ideation who are often suffering from mood disorders, substance abuse history and other social and mental disorders often present the therapist with the gravest threat of actually achieving a successful suicide (www.fda. gov). The capability of the client who has suicidal ideation should be assessed for the means to carry out the self-destructive threat, if the client has the means, then the risk is extremely high for a successful suicide. The psychiatrist on the practitioner's treatment team, perhaps, is in the best position to assess, analyze, and treat a client bent on committing suicide. Consult a psychiatrist who will often have hospital rights and privileges which augur well for a full range of examinations of the client including a complete physical and psychological assessment.

Various studies have indicated that the best way to prevent suicide is through the early recognition and treatment of depression and other psychiatric illnesses that lead to suicidal tendencies (AAS, 2005). Clients in a suicidal mode want to die by suicide can often be diagnosed as suffering from isolation, rejection and loneliness. They need the presence of a trusted friend, family member, therapist, who will listen and be there for them while depicting a caring demeanor. Often, these periodical depressive situations are often temporary, thus, death as a permanent solution is not warranted. Suicide is not about escaping the pain which seems at the moment unbearable. The illogical thought process of their private logic does not allow them to reason or see beyond the current pain or their disposition (Adler, A, 1961; Mosak, 1988). Encouragement, exploration of the meaning of life and coping skills often prove helpful depressed individuals with feelings of hurt, helplessness, lost and isolation.

In 2005 CDC (Center for Disease Control) stated that suicide was the eleventh leading cause of death in the U.S. and more that 32, 637 lives were lost to suicide(American Association of Suicidology, January 2, 2007). Major Depressive Disorders (MDD) was cited as the most prevalent mental health disorder associated with suicide. According to Kessler (2005 report that the lifetime risk of MDD was 16.6%; however Gotlib and Hammen (2002) indicated the rate was nearly 20%. These large numbers among the general population of U.S. citizenry seem not to have impacted the psychic mind of the larger population of the country since there has not been a demand for governmental programs to help reduce these numbers. However, in the mental health arena, these statistical data have long been known and studied, for impact has produced significant stressors upon practicing mental health providers. The famous and historical studies by both Deutsch (1984) and Farber (1983a) depicted their findings on stressful events that impacted practitioners the most were similar based therapist's descriptions of their stressors.

Deutsch's findings were in the following orders as to the most stressful behaviors that therapist had to manage:

1.   Suicidal statements
2.   Anger toward the therapist
3.   Severely depressed clients
4.   Apathy or lack of motivation
5.   Client's premature termination

Farber's findings were in listed in the following orders as to the most stressful behaviors that therapist had to manage:

1.   Suicidal statements
2.   Aggression and hostility
3.   Premature termination
4.   Agitated anxiety
5.   Apathy and depression

These classical studies provided proof of the stressful arena in which mental health practitioners work and indicate the high rate of professional burnout in this profession. To inoculate oneself from the effects of burnout, serious consideration must be given from the beginning of one's practice, to develop a proactive stress management program designed to keep the practitioner in a healthy and well-balanced state of physical and psychological health. In this effort Corey (2007) and Adler (1961) cited several areas of one personal life that ought to keep in balance they were: Spirituality, Friendship, Love, Work, and Self. Other authors (Mosak,

1998) added Family to this list of life tasks that must be carefully balanced for effective stress reduction and high productivity.

MANAGING CLIENTS WITH HIV/AIDS AND CONFIDENTIALITY

In the current level of social interactions on a world-wide perspective, a practitioner has a high probability of providing services for persons who have been tested and confirmed to be infected with the HIV virus. The documented increasing world-wide infection rate among all nations, present challenges to mental health practitioners in the delivery of effective therapeutic services and interventions in a confidential manner to this population. In the course of providing such services, practitioners must maintain confidentiality within the current legal and ethical structures of the profession or risk malpractice suits on legal issues. Confidentiality of clients health status, especially where infectious diseases are concerned such as the HIV virus, is critical and is legally binding upon therapists to conform. HIV/AIDS has the ability to affect a large portion of the U.S. population which contains many diverse groups.

Persons who have been tested and found to be HIV positive, are often stunned, confused, and feels isolated. This medical designation tends to separate such persons from the general population and label them with a stigma that is likely to change their style of life for ever. Such person often live in daily fear of recognition as an "AIDS person" which carries significant economical, social and political ramifications and death. Therefore, confidential processes and practices with such cases are critical in avoiding a malpractice lawsuit for unauthorized disclosure of such data. Additional training in this area is warranted due to the number of incidents and growing requirement for confidentiality in the maintenance of records over a seven (7) year period.

Corey et al, (2007) indicated that practitioners must have a clear vision of the limits of confidentiality, reporting requirements, laws of the state in which they practice, their duty to warn and to protect potential victims, and be able to communicate this information to their

HIV infected clients at the onset of the therapeutic process. If working with this population is beyond your training and skill levels, then such clients should be referred to more capable therapists. The practitioner must realize that ACA has not promulgated definitive guidelines for informing partners of such clients if the client refuses to share his/her HIV status with his sexual active partner. The practitioner may turn to the state laws in which he or she work for guidance, however, there is no common law among the several states of the U.S. which address this issue specifically and adequately.

There has been many recommendations to apply the Tarasoff decision to clients having unprotected sex with an unsuspecting partner and warning such partners without definitive success (Ahia & Martin, 1993; Erickson, 1993; Knapp & VandeCreek, 1990; Melchert & Patterson, 1999). Warning other persons about a client's HIV infection status is a very vexing, confusing and controversial issue. States response to this situation further confounds the responsibility to warn partners of HIV infected clients, for example, Texas does not abide by the Tarasoff decision, thus practitioners in that state has no responsibility to warn persons. The state of Pennsylvania forbade therapist from breaking confidentiality to warn potential victims of this potentially deadly disease. Only the state of Montana protect practitioners from liability when making disclosures in good faith to possible save ;another's life. Practitioners need to consult with their attorney, colleagues, and psychiatrist on your treatment team for guidance ensure that the "standard of care" is being upheld and maintained. Due care must be exercised so as not to inform persons who should <u>not</u> be informed, in each of these situations, clients may have a legal basis for suiting the therapist. Therefore, consultation and networking with more experiences colleagues is advised to avoid a malpractice suit.

The ACA ethic codes (2005) provide guidance on how to effectively manage clients and client's refusal stance in alerting partners to their proven HIV/AIDS (B.2.a.). The general requirement that practitioners keep information confidential does not apply when disclosure is required to protect clients or identified others from serious and foreseeable harm or when legal requirements demand that confidential information must be revealed. Practitioners consult with other professionals when in doubt as to the validity of an exception. Additional considerations apply when addressing end-of-life issues. B.2.a. (See A.9.c.).

Consultation or networking strategies might best be handled with the advice with a competent lawyer. The various states of the U.S. have developed their own statutes for dealing with client's infected with the HIV virus or full blown AIDS, who refuses to inform their sexual active partners of their status. As to contagious diseases disclosures to a partner who is engaged in unprotected sex with an HIV infected client, ACA ethic code provides the following guidance:

> When clients disclose that they have a disease commonly known to be both communicable and life threatening, practitioners <u>may</u> be justified in disclosing information to identifiable third parties, if they are known to be at demonstrable and high risk of contracting the disease. Prior to making a disclosure, practitioners confirm that there is such a diagnosis and assess the intent of clients to inform the third parties about their disease or to engage in any behaviors that may be harmful to an identifiable third party. B.2.b.

The author underlined and bolded <u>may</u> in the above state for emphasis. In this complex situation, ACA is found wanting for more specific guidance on this important subject to its members and to the mental health system at large.

SUMMARY

This chapter purported to provide an overview of some of the major issues likely to confront a practitioner beginning his/her career in the mental health field. The content of this chapter covered briefly the following concepts: the importance of a well-development of an informed consent document and the delineation of one's theoretical stance for therapy. The chapter outlined the process highly recommended for making ethical decisions when little or guidance is provided in the literature. The major differences between confidentiality, privileged communication and privacy were noted.

REFERENCES

Adler, A. (H.L. Ansbacher, Ed.). (1969). *The science of living*. Doubleday.

Adler, A. (1930). *Social Interest*. New York, Capricorn Books, 1964.

Adler, A. (1931). *What Life Should Mean to You*. New York, Capricorn Books, 1958.

Ahia, D.E., & Martin, D. (1993). T*he danger-to-self-or-others exception to confidentiality*. Alexandria, VA: American Counseling Association. American Association for Marriage and Family Therapy (2001).

American Association of Suicidology, January 2, 2007. *Major Depressive Disorders*.

American Association of Suicidology, January 21, 2008. *Suicide in the U.S.A. based on Current (2005) Statistics*.

American Counseling Association (1997). *Code of ethics and standards of practice*. Alexandria, VA.

Bashham, A., & O»Conner, M. (2005). In C. S. Cashwell & J. S. Young, (eds.) *Integrating spirituality and religion into counseling: A guide to competent practice* (pp. 143–167). Alexandria, VA: American Counseling Association.

Belaire, C., Young, J. S., & Ekder, A. (2005) Inclusion of religious behaviors and attitudes in counseling: Expectations of conservative Christians. *Counseling and Values*, 49(2). 82–94.

Bemak, F., & Chung, R. C-Y. (2004). Teaching multicultural group counseling: perspectives by a new era. *Journal for Specialists in Group Work*, 29(1), 31–41.

Bennett, B.E., Bryant, B.K., VanderBos, G.R., & Greenwood, A. (1990). *Professional liability and risk management*. Washington, D.C.: American Psychological Association.

Benitez, B. R. (2004). Confidentiality and its exceptions. *The Therapist*, 16(4), 32–36.

Bersoff, D. (1999). *Ethical conflicts in psychology* (2nd ed.). Washington, D.C.: American Psychological Association.

Boisvert, C. M., & Faust, D. (2003). Leading researchers' consensus on psychotherapy research findings: Implications for the teaching and conduct of psychotherapy. *Professional Psychology: Research and Practice*, 34(5), 508–513.

Campbell, C. D., & Gordon, M. C. (2003). Acknowledging the inevitable: Understanding multiple relationships in rural practices. *Professional Psychology: Research and Practice*, 34(4), 430–434.

Capuzzi, D. (Ed.) (2004). *Suicide across the life span: Implications for counselors.* Alexandria, VA: American Counseling Association.

CDC (Center for Disease Control) 2005

Cobia, D.C. and Pipes, R. B. (2002). Mandated supervision: An intervention for disciplined professionals. *Journal of Counseling and Development,* 80, 140–144.

Corey, M. S. and Callahan, P. (2007) *Issues and ethics in the helping profession Pacific* (7ᵗʰ ed.). Grove, Ca.: Brooks/Cole Publishing Company.

Deutsch, C. J. (1984). Self-reported sources of stress among psychotherapists. *Professional Psychology*, 15, 833–845.

Erickson, S. H. (1993). Ethics and confidentiality in AIDS counseling: A professional dilemma. *Journal of Mental Health Counseling*, 15(2), 118–131.

Farber, B. A. (1983). *Stress and burnout in the human services professions.* (Ed.). New York: Pregamon Press.

Farber, B. A. (1983). The effects of psychotherapeutic practice upon psychotherapists. *Psychotherapy*, 20, 174–183.

Gladding, S. (1992). *Counseling as an art: The creative arts in counseling.* Alexandria, VA. American Counseling Association.

Gladding, Samuel T. (1992). *Counseling: A comprehensive profession.* (2ⁿᵈ ed.). New York, New York: Macmillan Publishing Company.

Herlihy, B., & Corey, G. (1996b). Confidentiality. In B. Herlihy & G. Corey. (Eds), *ACA ethical standards casebook* (5th ed.) (pp. 205–209). Alexandria, VA: American Counseling Association

Huber, C. H. and Baruth L. G. (2007). *Ethical, legal and professional issues in the practice of marriage and family therapy* (4ᵗʰ ed.). Merrill Publishing Company.

Kessler, E.C., Berglund, P., Demler, O., Lin, R., &Walters, E. E. (2005). Lifetime prevalence and age-of-onset distribution of DSM-IV disorders in National Co morbidity Survey Replication. *Archives of General Psychiatry*, 62, p. 593.

Knapp, S. &VandeCreek, L. (1990). Application of the duty to protect to HIV-positive patients. *Professional Psychology: Research and Practice* 21(3), 161–166.

Lakin, Martin (1991). *Coping with ethical dilemmas in psychotherapy.* Pergamon Press.

Maslach, C. (1986). Stress, burnout, and workaholism. In Kilburg, R. R., Nathan, P. E., & Thoreson, R. & W. (Eds.). *Professionals in distress: Issues, syndromes, and solutions in psychology*. Washington D.C.: American Psychological Association.

Maslach, C. (1993). Burnout: A multidimensional perspective. In Schaufeli, W. B., Maslach, C., & Marek, T. (Eds.). *Professional burnout: recent developments in theory and research* (pp. 19–32). Washington, DC: Taylor & Francis.

Maslach, C. (2003). Job burnout: New directions in research and intervention. *Current Directions in Psychological Science*, 12, 189–192.

Maslach, C. (2005). Understanding burnout: Work and family issues. In D. F. Halpern & S. E. Murphy (Eds.), *From work-family balance to work-family interaction: Changing the metaphor* (99–114). Mahwah, NJ : Lawrence Erlbaum.

Melchert, T. P. & Patterson, M. M (1999). Duty to warn and interventions with HIV-positive clients. *Professional Psychology: Research and Practice*, 30(2), 180–186.

Moline, M. E, Williams, G. T., & Austin, K. M. (1997) *Documenting psychotherapy: essentials for mental health practitioners*. SAGE Publishers.

Ohlschlager, G., & Mosgofian, P. (1992). *Law for the Christian counselor: A guidebook for clinicians and pastors*. Dallas: Word Books.

Pope, K.S., & Vasquez, M.J.T. (1991). *Ethics in psychotherapy and counseling: A practical guide for psychologists*. San Francisco: Jossey-Bass.

Shulman, B. and Mosak, H. (1988). *Manual for life style assessment*. Accelerated Development, Accelerated Development, Inc.

Truscott, D., & Evans, J. (2001). Responding to dangerous clients. In E.R. Welfel & E. Ingersonn (Eds.). *The mental health desk reference: A sourcebook for counselors and therapists* (pp. 271–276). New York: Wiley.

Truscott, D., Evans, J., Mansell, S. (1995). Outpatient psychotherapy with dangerous clients: A model for clinical decision making. *Professional Psychology: Research and Practice*, 26, 484–490. [Reprinted in D. N. Bersoff (Ed.). (2003). Ethical conflicts in psychology (3rd ed.). Washington, DC:

Sapienza, B. G., & Bugental, J. F.T (2000). Keeping our instruments finely tuned: An existential-humanistic perspective. *Professional Psychology: Research and Practice*, 31(4), 458–460.

Swanson, L. C., (1979). *Psychology and law for the helping professions*. Pacific Grove, CA: Brooks/Cole.

USPSTF Web site (http://www.preventiveservices.ahrq.gov).

So You Want to Earn a Doctorate

11

By Rhonda Jeter-Twilley, Ph.D.

A personal account and advice for students interested in pursuing doctoral studies in counseling and psychology.

This chapter will look at a variety of issues related to pursuing a doctorate. There are three sections in the chapter, Consider the End at the Beginning, Personal Issues to consider before deciding to work on a Doctorate, and Academic Issues in Selecting a Program/Questions You Should Know to Ask. The information contained in this chapter will hopefully be helpful as you consider this career option.

CONSIDER THE END AT THE BEGINNING

So, you think you want to go on for a doctorate. The idea of becoming a doctor is grand, exciting, and lofty. The thought of hearing them call you Dr. _____ can fill you with pride and make you tingle all over. But before you sign up for a doctoral program, any doctoral program, there are some major things you need to consider and some major questions that need to asked.

Because I am a chair in a counseling department, not a week goes by when a student does not stop by or call to ask about how to go about becoming a doctor. My first question is always the same. Why do you want to become a doctor? While this question may seem simple and trite, it is the quintessential query that will assist you in deciding if a doctorate is for you. Moreover, if you decide you do want or need a doctorate to meet your personal or career goals, this question will also assist you in thinking about the kind of doctorate that will help you meet those goals. So, thinking about the end (your ultimate goal) at the beginning really makes a lot of sense.

The responses I have received to the question, "Why do you want to become a doctor?" are interesting and varied. I am going to discuss two of the most common responses that I often hear. One response is "I want to be able to have a private practice. Don't I need a doctorate to do that?" The short answer to this question is no, but the long response to this question opens up a conversation about licensure. Because people know that Psychologists and Psychiatrists sometimes have private practices, it is sometimes assumed that you must have a doctorate to do so. Many master's level counselors have private practices. The major issue for having a private practice is whether you have a license from your state. Psychologists, Psychiatrists, Counselors, Nurses, Social Workers, and Family Therapists are some of the major types of mental health professionals that can acquire a license from the state. Each license has specific parameters that most be met in terms of education, coursework, examinations, internship experiences, and hours worked in the field under supervision. Receiving a license also gives you access to using professional titles protected by the state. For example, any one can call themselves a counselor, but the term Licensed Professional Counselor (LPC) is a protected title. While the term may vary slightly in different states, people using a licensed title without receiving a license are legally at risk.

In my state, people seeking to obtain a license (a) must receive a master's degree (b) must have a total of 60 credit hours which must include course work in specific required areas (c) pass the National Counselors Exam (d) 3000 hours of supervised work experience (d) pass a brief state law exam (Maryland Department of Health and Mental Hygiene, 2009). You should check the licensure procedure in your state. Once obtaining a license you can submit to receive 3rd party payments from insurance companies, advertise using the protected title, and have a private practice. Even if you went on for a doctorate, you would still have to apply for licensure by meeting your state's requirements for that profession in order to have a private practice. While not optimal, one could even have a private practice without a license, but it means only being able to receive payments directly from the clients. Most clients cannot afford to pay much if they have to do so without the assistance of insurance. Also, you will be competing with people who are credential by the state. Thus, if you were seeking a doctorate for the purpose of opening a private practice, then a doctorate is not necessary. Are there advantages to having a private practice after attaining a doctorate? Yes, there are a few. While it is still advisable to apply for license, clients sometimes seek out a therapist with doctorate. You can also charge more for your services if you have more expanded education and skills gained under supervision. If you train in a specific area such as psychology, you can only call yourself a psychologist if you have the degree and the license.

In sum, you can have a private practice as a respected, licensed professional at the master's level. A doctorate with several years of coursework and a dissertation can add value as mentioned above, but it is not as critical as having a license in being able to have a successful private practice.

The other popular response that I receive to the question of "Why do you want a doctorate" is that I have always wanted to be a doctor." If this is your major objective, then you have the greatest amount of flexibility. There are many types of doctorates, and a variety of fields. Some with more credibility than others. Most people do not know the difference. I would always recommend getting a doctorate from an accredited university. It is harder to get universal acceptance and be able to use your credits towards licensure and other types of professional recognition when the doctorate is from an unaccredited university. While this will be discussed in more detail later in the chapter, if you do not have a career goal where you need a doctorate in a specific area, then any doctorate in any field will do. Some students opt for a doctorate in a field they are not interested in because it is available or quick to obtain. If you get a degree in Educational Leadership or Religious Studies, then you are technically an expert in that area. You would not be eligible in most universities to teach counseling just because your master's degree is in that area. If you ultimately want to teach counseling or psychology, you will need a doctoral degree in that area. Additionally, academe is an area where credentials are routinely scrutinized. Where your get your degree, what academic area you obtain it in, the accreditation of your college, and traditionally vs. non-traditional programs can be an issue. So, if you want to interface with universities after you receive a doctorate, you need to consider this when you make your final decision regarding your program. For example, I worked at one university where a student from my master's program got a 2–year doctorate from an unaccredited religious college. After she got her degree, she wanted to be called "DR." People in the outside world addressed her as so, but at the administration at the university where she worked as support staff, prohibited her from using the title. If your objective is just to be called "DR." and you have no plans to work at a mainstream college or university, then a degree from any place will do.

PH.D., ED.D, & PSY.D—WHAT'S THE DIFFERENCE?

While there are several doctorates in related areas which will be discussed later in this chapter, this section will focus on three types of Doctorates—the Doctorate of Philosophy (Ph.D.), the Doctorate of Education (Ed.D.) and the Doctorate of Psychology (Psy.D). There used to be clear cut delineations among these three areas. This section will give the traditional ways these have been defined. However, these degrees may vary from university to university in the way they are defined or viewed. So it is important to check how each program you are considering defines these degree types.

The Doctor of Philosophy, Ph.D. is generally considered a research based degree. In the traditional frame, it is considered the higher more lofty degree type (Merriam-Webster Online Dictionary, 2009). A Ph.D. is concerned more prestigious because of it focus on research rather than application. A person can have a Ph.D. in many academic areas. In the fields of counseling and psychology, a person who gets the degree is considered to have both research and applied skills. A person with a Ph.D. in psychology could have a career as an academic, or as practitioner or as an academic and a practitioner. During commencement at my in the university where I received my doctorate, Ph.D. candidates across all programs received their degrees at one time, and they were called first. All of the applied degree candidates were called later with their discipline. Some students select the Ph.D. because they were aware of this distinction.

Ph.D. classes may cost more than Ed.D classes at some universities. At the university I attended, the major difference between the Ph.D. degree and the Ed.D. degree was the cost. Ph.D. candidates paid more for the classes than Ed.D. candidates. This is not true at every university. At some universities the number of research and statistics courses varies or there are some other differences. The meaning of Ph.D. and Ed.D. can vary sharply depending on where attend. One just needs to inquiry about the degree types at the university you plan attend.

Ph.D. programs generally have more of a research emphasis. Dissertations tend to be experimental or quasi-experimental, and original research is used. Programs may have additional statistics and research courses in order strengthened candidate's research background. Unlike other Ph.D. programs, those in psychology or counseling also required candidates to complete a year-long full-time internship. This prepares them to ultimately be practitioners as well as researchers. This makes the completion of a traditional Ph.D. program in Counseling or Psychology a year longer than PhD's in other content areas. When considering schools for admissions, review the Ph.D. program's components. If you are not interested in a research-based degree, you might want to consider the Ed.D. or a Psy.D.

The Doctor of Education (Ed.D) is usually a degree that focuses on preparation of competent professionals with a foundation in theory and knowledge of policy to practice in the field (Merriam-Webster Online Dictionary, 2009). People who pursue these degrees often become leaders in the field of education and are prepared to identify solutions to complex educational issues by applying theory and research. The Ed. D. was first granted from Harvard in 1920. It was created to respond to the need for more people in the field of education to have doctoral level degrees. Many fields have degrees that focus on practice more so than research (JD, MD, D.DIV to name a few). So a Doctorate in Education was created. How does this relate to counseling and psychology? Unlike clinical psychology programs which tend to be housed in Psychology Departments, many counseling programs, and most Counseling Psychology Programs are housed in Schools and Colleges of Education. Thus, many Colleges or Schools of Education offer and Ed.D. in Counseling Psychology, Counseling or Counselor Education and Supervision. Others offer both the Ph.D. and Ed.D. options. Those that offer the Ed.D. often have an emphasis on preparing practitioners, however these programs have some emphasis on research. Other colleges and schools with Ed.D.'s in Counseling Psychology, Counseling, or Counselor Education and Supervision prepare the student to practice and engage in research. Programs vary sharply from a reduced emphasis on research, to use of action research, to having the identical requirements that traditional Ph.D. programs require. Before you select an Ed.D. program, be sure to examine the components to see if the requirements and emphasis meets your ultimate goal. Both Ed.D. s and Ph.D.'s can teach at the college level, but if you are looking for less coursework in research and statistics, you may be looking for an Ed.D in Counseling or Psychology or Counselor Education and Supervision.

A Doctor of Psychology, (Psy.D). is actually a professional doctorate in Clinical Psychology (Norcross, Sayette & Mayne, 2008). This degree is relatively new. It was created in 1973 at a psychology conference in Vail. The objective was to open an additional avenue for becoming a clinical psychologist that would focus on the preparing a professionals for a wide range of practitioner roles in the field. The traditional route, Ph.D. in Clinical Psychology prepares a person for research and practice. Whereas the Psy.D. was created to be a practitioner's degree. These programs tend to have less research and statistics courses than their traditional counterpart. Some of them have research papers or dissertations that focus on practical research instead of the traditional dissertation format. A Ph.D. or Ed.D program in Counseling or Clinical Psychology would require a one year internship. Psy.D. Program often has two years of internship or augmented clinical experiences. Both programs take 4–7 years to complete. Anyone with a doctorate in Clinical Psychology, Counseling Psychology or a Psy.D. is eligible to be licensed as a Psychologist in every state. Graduates with a Psy.D hold positions in venues such as clinics, hospitals, businesses, schools, public and private institutions, research, administration and academe. Ph.D.'s will usually have more options in academe because of their research training. Initially, the Psy.D. was not well accepted, but it has gained in popularity and respect in the field, and is now a popular option. In terms of finances there tends to be more assistantships for Ph.D. programs than in Psy.D. programs because of the research assistant needs associated with these programs.

Overall, it is important that you understand your options at the beginning so that you will have a degree that meets your career goals.

CLINICAL PSYCHOLOGY, COUNSELING PSYCHOLOGY, AND COUNSELOR EDUCATION: WHAT'S THE DIFFERENCE?

Most people know what a Clinical Psychologist does. It is the traditional psychologist we often see on TV in a book, or in person at a hospital or private practice. Clinical Psychologists teach, research or treat mental health issues of a severe or chronic nature, such as schizophrenia or a bipolar disorder. Often these clients are seen as "sick" and needing long-term or serious intervention. In terms of training, Clinical Psychologists receive training to become experts in assessment as well as psychotherapy. Often their internships are in hospitals or mental health inpatient or forensic settings. Often people confuse Clinical Psychologists with Psychiatrists, who are MD's which also work with clients with serious mental health issues, but they focus on the biological bases of the dysfunctional behavior and often prescribe medication. Clinical Psychologists have the highest status in the psychology field. In a few states they can take specialized training to prescribe medication.

Counseling Psychologists are psychological specialists whose training prepares them to work with clients with less severe, everyday stressors (Norcross, Sayette & Mayne, 2008). Their clients are generally psychologial healthy people who are having some distress or are stuck. While there is overlap in training so they can deal with some serious issues, they focus on problems related to career, relationship, developmental, educational, social and emotional concerns, and crisis. Interventions tend to alleviate distress and help clients lead more satisfying and productive lives. When I was trying to get into the field, I was told that people only majored in Counseling Psychology who could not get into a Clinical Psychology Programs. Personally, Counseling Psychology was my 1st choice because I like to work with clients who have normal, everyday problems and who with intervention get better and move ahead. You will find them working with a wide variety of areas such as health psychology, substance abuse, adult development, family psychology, group process, crisis intervention, eating disorders, and anxiety disorders just to name a few. A person with a doctorate in Counseling Psychology is eligible for licensure as a Psychologist and as a Counselor (Conway, 1988).

The doctorate in Counselor Education or Counselor Education and Supervision is for students in the field of Counseling who want to get a terminal degree. Students with School Counseling Degrees, Mental Heath Counseling Degrees, Community Counseling Degrees and other counseling areas can seek a degree in Counselor Education. Most of these programs are housed in College or Schools of Education. There is a great deal of overlap between training in Counseling Psychology and Counselor Education. More and more, departments of Counselor Education are seeking people with terminal degrees in this field. Since this is a relatively new area, they often hire those in related areas such as psychology, but as the field is growing, they are seeking to emphasis a counselor identity that is separate from psychology. Students with a doctoral degree in Counselor Education can be licensed at the master's level or the doctoral level as a counselor. However, because this is not a psychology degree one cannot apply for psychology licensure. It must be counseling.

RELATED FIELDS: DOCTORATE IN FAMILY THERAPY, DOCTORATE IN SOCIAL WORK
Doctorate in Family Therapy

Family Therapy is a related field that prepares students to do work with families from a family system's perspective. This is considered a specialty area in the field of counseling. Students can enter some doctoral programs in Family Therapy without a master's degree in Family Therapy, as long as you have a master's degree in a related area. Some states have licensure specifically for family therapists. After taking a family therapy class during their counseling programs, some students decide that they want to work with problems from a family systems perspective. Perhaps a doctorate in Family Counseling or Family Therapy might be the most appropriate choice for you.

Doctorate in Social Work

Unlike Family Therapy, in order to pursue a doctorate in Social Work, you will need a master's in Social Work. There are Doctorates in Social Work DSW's and Ph.D.'s in Social Work. In most programs these degree designations are interchangeable because the degree prepares you for research, clinical practice, and administration. Social Work has many specialty areas one of which is clinical. Some Social Workers have counseling or clinical training, and like counselors they can be licensed at the master's level. In the future you may see more DSW programs focusing on practice and Ph.D. programs focusing on research.

ASPECTS FOR CONSIDERATION PRIOR TO STARTING YOUR DOCTORAL PROGRAM

It is critical to consider several key aspects of your life before starting your doctoral program, if your ultimate goal is to exit successfully from your program with your degree in hand. Many doctoral students that are "All But Dissertation" (ABD) failed to plan for one or several of these critical life elements, which ultimately influence their achievement in their doctoral program. Considering these critical life elements prior to starting your doctoral program will save you time and decrease problems later. The critical life elements that you should consider include family responsibilities, social ties, professional responsibilities, personal time and finances. Many doctoral students that do not finish or remain ABD do not plan to fail; they fail to plan for the successful completion of their degree.

Family Responsibilities

Prior to starting your first class as a doctoral student, you must consider what supports your family needs addressed and how things will need to shift if you are to be successful. If you have young children, who will care for them while you are in class? Who will provide back up care for your children? What if your child has special projects for school or is involved in sports? Supports need to be identified and put into place so that you are not undermined at the start of your program. Sometimes children have unique issues; these issues must be successfully addressed if you are to complete your program. I had a friend that started her doctoral program at the same time that I started mine. Her child had a severe behavioral disorder, which required my friend to constantly interact with the school. My friend did not identify any one to support her or her child during these points of crisis even though her child had a history of difficulty. She withdrew from the program after the first semester. She failed to plan. She may have had a different outcome had she considered the supports that her child needed and put them into place prior to entering her doctoral program.

Another family issue that some need to consider is the timetable for starting a family. Many times I have seen students start a program and also and decide to start a family during that time. Because they had not planned for all of the changes that pregnancy and a new child can add to their life, it has caused some to major delay or permanently derail completing a doctoral degree. Discussing and deciding overall life goals as they relate to your working on a doctorate will assist you in putting a plan in place that will make it more possible to complete your degree.

Besides children, one must consider spouses, partners, and parents. Few of us are isolated from family responsibilities, so consideration of your new or reduce roles and interactions must be considered. You may need to schedule date nights with your spouse or partner. You may not be able to call or go to your parents' house daily as in the past. Sit down and discuss wherever possible with the people you love about these critical changes. You may not make all the family functions or cook the traditional family dinners for the next few years. Try to assist the family in identifying others that can take on new roles and responsibilities. Explain to them that these changes will not be forever but will support your in achieving your goal. Be clear.

Social Ties

Friends, we all have them. You must consider your friendships before beginning your doctoral program. How much time will you be able to spend with your friends? What will you miss? How will you explain the changes in the amount of availability that you have to interact with them? I belonged to a book club prior to starting my doctoral program. I read the books and participated in the book club bi-monthly. As I entered my doctoral program, I told my friends that I might not be able to read the assigned books. They all agreed that was "ok" and that I should come as a break or stress reliever. Initially, I came regularly but as time went on and my program demanded more of my time, I began to miss book club meetings. I think the last year of my program, I did not attend one, but I always called or responded to the emails so they knew I was interested and thinking of them, but could not attend. This helped me to maintain my network of supports while focusing on my studies. Make time for friends, but you must decide that school is a priority if you are to reach your goal. Ultimately, they may still not understand, but having these conversations ahead of time will help.

Professional Responsibilities

Balancing your program with your career can be difficult. Consider any changes in your professional responsibilities during your doctoral program very carefully. A change in your level or kind of professional responsibilities may possibility derail you from completing your program in a timely fashion or entirely. A good friend of mine started her program a year behind me. She received a fabulous job offer. She took the job and changed her career. She decided after the third semester of her doctoral program to take an indefinite leave of absence from the program because her new professional responsibilities were overwhelming.

Finances

If you are the designee in your household to pay the bills you may need a support person or another system, if you want to maintain your credit rating throughout the doctoral program. Sometimes your increasingly busy schedule could cause you to forget to make scheduled payments. Another support that you could institute is the automatic bank draft system that many financial institutions now offer which pays your bills on set days each month. Financial planning is an important consideration that one must ponder r prior to enrolling in a doctoral program. Failing to plan financially could have serious repercussions which could delay the completion of your program. For doctoral students that are dependent on student loans, be aware of the date each year that you must submit your Free Application for Federal Student Aid forms (FAFSA). A late submission could affect your eligibility for loans. The best advice is to stay informed about dates and deadlines concerning your student aid.

If possible, seek scholarships that may be offered by your current employer or through your spouse or partners employer. In some instances, doctoral students that are working as adjunct professors or graduate assistants and residential directors, may have a portion or all of their courses paid for by the university. You should explore all possibilities that could enhance or decrease the cost of you obtaining your doctoral degree.

Lastly, you need to take into account the extraneous expenses related to working on a dissertation. Using a dissertation coach, a statistical consultant, an APA editor, multiple copies, binding, final copies, copyrighting, refreshments for the defense etc., can really add up. Some students I have worked with have estimated that they spent as much as $ 4,000 while completing their dissertation. This was a financial stressor because they had no idea about the cost associated with completing the dissertation.

Building a Network of Support

One of the most important aspects to consider prior to entering your chosen doctoral program is the web of support that you will need. Your support base needs to include individuals and resources that can enhance your overall experience and will be used to assist you in achieving your overall goal of completing your doctoral degree.

You may need to identify a person or persons that can read your papers after you have written them. Many days when papers and projects are due, you may need a person to review your work for errors in grammar. The person or persons that you choose should be well versed in English grammar. Sometimes you can identify a person at your place of employment or a person from inside your social network. Many universities have a writing center that you may be able to access for support. This is a great resource but they are only available at certain times and you often need to complete a paper well in advance.

In the event that you do not have a resource available or you are a person that waits until you have time to complete a project, you may need to connect with an editor that you pay. There are many options available on the internet but you do have to screen carefully the prospective editors. You want an experienced editor with several references that you can contact for confirmation of this person's level of expertise. You also want someone who is well versed in American

Psychological Association (APA) citations and formatting. This can save you a great deal of time and anxiety if your editor is also an APA specialist. Identifying this person prior to entering your program will give you a great sense of self-confidence that you have support where you access it or not.

In addition to the program support, build a strong connection with someone that can become your emotional support point person. You need someone that will just listen to you as you vent or discuss your challenges as they relate to your program. This person will neither critique you or what you say but who is simply there on your side for the long haul in front of you. This person will be your lifeboat on the days that you think you are drowning and cannot make it. This person is often quintessential to you ultimately achieving your degree. Remember this person may not always understand what you are saying but he or she is there for you.

ACADEMIC ISSUES IN SELECTING A PROGRAM/ QUESTIONS YOU SHOULD KNOW TO ASK.

There some questions you need to ask before selecting the program where you will complete your doctoral study. Regardless of the university, each program has strengths and weaknesses. Some people assume if you select a top tier university, then all of the programs will be great, but this is not necessarily so. Asking these questions will let you know about the quality of the program, and help you avoid unexpected problems that could keep you from finishing in a timely fashion. This section of the chapter will raise questions and respond with things you should ask about in order to find a program that is a good fit for you.

Question 1—Is the program Traditional or Non-Traditional?

A traditional program in the psychology or counseling is generally full-time and may meet during the day. A traditional program could take 4–7 years to finish. Remember in the Counseling and Psychology fields, you have at least one year of internship in addition to your coursework and dissertation. Traditional programs generally have Comprehensives Exams, and Advancement to Candidacy requirements.

A non-traditional program tends to be missing one or more of the components listed above, or could meet at night or on the weekend, or totally on-line. A non-tradition program may not require comprehensive exams and may use an alternative to a traditional dissertation. Some non-traditional programs are designed to assist students in completing the programs in a timely fashion. If you need a non-traditional format, then be sure to look for these parameters.

Question 2—Does the program require an Entrance Exam or Not?

Many schools require an entrance exam such as the GRE or the MAT. Some programs only require that you take them, but do not designate a cut off score. Others have a specific cut-off score or require a minimal GPA. There are schools that have a cut off date for the age of the scores, and some that do not require scores at all. If testing is not your forte, you should look for a school where this is not as much of an issue.

Question 3—Does the program use a Cohort Model or a Traditional Model?

It is important to ask whether the program uses a cohort model or a traditional model. Some programs use a cohort model which admits a certain number of people that become a group. They take all of their classes together, all take the same number of classes, have the same professors, and reach the milestones in the program at the same time. A traditional model admits students for the program, but students determine how many classes they will take, which professors, at how quickly they will matriculate through the program. The advantages of a cohort program is that you have people going through the experience all together so there is the potential for support, everyone has the notes if you miss class, you get to know who to work with on projects. Conversely, there is the potential for competition. If there is a personality conflict there is little escape. Generally there is only one section of the class offered, so you cannot change to another professor if you are having difficulty with his or her teaching style. If you need to take time off for personal or professional reasons, it makes it more difficult to complete your program and disconnects you from your original cohort.

Question 4—Are you considering a Full-time or a Part-time Program?

Most traditional programs are full-time. If you are in the position to attend a full-time program, there are some advantages to being able to spend time in your department and to be able to focus full-time on your degree. For most students, attending full-time requires financial support from family or a graduate assistantship. Part-time programs are built around the fact that most students work. It takes longer to complete the degree, but you are able to work a full-time position and complete your degree. Online programs can usually be paced to work around a full-time work schedule and may accelerate your pace.

Question 5—What kind of accreditation does the program have?

Not all programs are accredited, but high quality programs usually are. There are of course exceptions to this rule. For example, some Ivy League College Counseling Programs do not have accreditation. The American Psychological Association (APA) accredits Psychology programs, and Council for the Accreditation of Counseling and Related Education Programs (CACREP) accredits Counseling Programs. Family Therapy Programs are accredited by American Association of Marriage and Family Therapist (AAMFT).

Question 6—Who are the faculty and what are their research interests?

When you are looking for doctoral programs, reviewing your options for advising and for your dissertation chairperson are important factors to consider. Questions that you should ask concerning the programs you are considering include, how many staff members have tenure and how long have they been with the program? You want to know that the person that you may potentially choose to be your dissertation chair is going to be there throughout your tenure in the program. Other questions to consider include, what is the range of research interests in the department? How many students do they admit each year? What is the matriculation rate for students entering the program? What are the supports available to assist students in completing their degrees? How many of the students publish an article or do a professional presentation prior to graduation? Is there a list of graduates that you could speak with that could share their experiences of the program? These questions and others will provide clarification about the program and if this is the program for you.

Question 7—Does the Program Have Comprehensive Exams?

Most traditional programs do have Comprehensive Exams. Some programs have preliminary exams, that have to be taken early in the program and Comprehensive Exams later in the program. One can spend several months preparing for these exams. Comprehensive Exams can last for several days covering different aspects of the program. Some non-traditional programs do not have Comprehensive Exams. Students are assessed in other ways. If testing is not your strong suit, you might look for a program that does not have Comprehensive Exams.

Question 8—Is a Dissertation Required for the program?

Once again, traditional programs usually have dissertations. You must demonstrate your research skills and use of theory, while working through original research. Some non-traditional programs require a research paper, other a final project rather than a dissertation. The dissertation process can be time-consuming and expensive. So, if you find a program that does not require a traditional dissertation, it could speed up the process of completing your degree.

REFERENCES

Conway, J. B. (1988). Differences among clinical psychologists: Scientists, practitioners, and scientist–practitioners. *Professional Psychology: Research and Practice, 19,* 642–655.

Ed.D. (2009). In *Merriam-Webster Online Dictionary*. Retrieved May 20, 2009, from http://www.merriam-webster.com/dictionary/EdD.

Maryland Department of Health and Mental Hygiene. (2009). *Professional Counselor Licensure Requirements (LCPC)*. Required May 23, 2009, from the Maryland Department of Health and Mental Hygiene Website://dhmh.state.md.us/bopcweb/html/profcounselor.htm.

Norcross, J., Sayette, M., & Mayne, T. (2008). Insider's guide to graduate programs in clinical and counseling psychology: 2008/2009 edition. New York: Guilford Press.

PhD. (2009). In *Merriam-Webster Online Dictionary*. Retrieved May 20, 2009, from http://www.merriam-webster.com/dictionary/PhD.